Thematic Unit

Archaeology

Written by Mary Ellen Sterling

Teacher Created Materials, Inc.
6421 Industry Way
Westminster, CA 92683
www.teachercreated.com

©1994 Teacher Created Materials, Inc.
Reprinted, 2002

Made in U.S.A.

ISBN 1-55734-296-2

Illustrations by
Blanca Apodaca La Bounty

Cover Art by
Kathy Bruce

Table of Contents

Introduction

Archaeology contains a comprehensive whole language, thematic unit. Its 80 reproducible pages are filled with a wide variety of lesson ideas designed for use with intermediate and middle school students. At its core are two high-quality reading selections, *The Usborne Young Scientist: Archaeology* and *Dig This! How Archaeologists Uncover Our Past.*

For each of these books, activities are included which set the stage for reading, encourage the enjoyment of the book, and extend the concepts. Activities are also provided that integrate the curriculum areas of language arts (including writing and research skills), math, science, social studies, art, music, and life skills. Many of these activities are conducive to the use of cooperative learning groups.

Suggestions and patterns for bulletin boards and unit management tools are additional time savers for the busy teacher. Furthermore, directions for student-created Big Books and a culminating activity, which allow students to synthesize their knowledge in order to produce products that can be shared beyond the classroom, highlight this very complete teacher resource.

This thematic unit includes:

literature selections—summaries of two books with related lessons that cross the curriculum

planning guides—suggestions for sequencing lessons of the unit

writing ideas—daily writing suggestions and activities that cross the curriculum, including Big Books and Picture Books

bulletin boards—suggestions and plans for content related and interactive bulletin boards

home/school connections—for extending the unit to the student's home

curriculum connections—in language arts, math, science, social studies, art, music, and life skills

group projects—to foster cooperative learning

culminating activities—which require students to synthesize their learning and participate in activities that can be shared with others

a bibliography—suggesting additional literature and nonfiction books relating to this unit

---

To keep this valuable resource intact so that it can be used year after year you may wish to punch holes in the pages and store them in a three-ring binder.

Introduction *(cont.)*

Why Whole Language?

A whole language approach involves children in using all modes of communication: reading, writing, listening, observing, illustrating, experiencing, and doing. Communication skills are interconnected and integrated into lessons that emphasize the whole of language rather than isolating its parts. The lessons revolve around selected literature. Reading is not taught as a subject separate from writing and spelling, for example. A child reads, writes, speaks, listens, and thinks in response to a literature experience introduced by the teacher. In this way, language skills grow naturally, stimulated by involvement and interest in the topic at hand.

Why Thematic Planning?

One very useful tool for implementing an integrated whole language program is thematic planning. By choosing a theme with correlating literature selections for a unit of study, a teacher can plan activities throughout the day that lead to a cohesive, in-depth study of the topic. Students will be practicing and applying their skills in meaningful contexts. Consequently, they will tend to learn and retain more. Both teachers and students will be freed from a day that is broken into unrelated segments of isolated drill and practice.

Why Cooperative Learning?

Besides academic skills and content, students need to learn social skills. No longer can this area of development be taken for granted. Students must learn to work cooperatively in groups in order to function well in modern society. Group activities should be a regular part of school life and teachers should consciously include social objectives as well as academic objectives in their planning. The teacher should clarify and monitor the qualities of good group interaction, just as he/she would clarify and monitor the academic goals of the project.

Why Big Books?

An excellent cooperative, whole language activity is the production of Big Books. Groups of students or the whole class, can apply their language skills, content knowledge, and creativity to produce a Big Book that can become a part of the classroom library to be read and reread. These books make excellent culminating projects for sharing beyond the classroom with parents, librarians, and others. Big Books can be produced in many ways, and this thematic unit book includes directions for several methods you may choose.

The Usborne Young Scientist: Archaeology

by Barbara Cork and Struan Reid

Summary

Here is a book that can be used as a supplemental or introductory tool for an in-depth study of archaeology. Its pages are chock full of information about archaeologists and how they search for clues to the past; how these clues are pieced together; the importance of pottery, animal, and plant remains; how the age of artifacts is determined; and even how underwater explorations have provided insights into our past. Colorful illustrations and diagrams abound, enhancing the text.

The text itself is broken down into manageable bits of information. The layout of the pictures and text combine to make it easy to find sub-topics.

A glossary of terms employed throughout the pages completes the book. The Usborne Young Scientist: Archaeology *serves as a stimulating springboard for motivating students to learn more about the many facets of archaeology.*

The outline below is a suggested plan for using the various activities that are presented in this unit. You should adapt these ideas to fit your own classroom situation.

Sample Plan

Lesson I
- Set up an archaeology center (page 6).
- Read a coin (page 17).
- Assign pages for reading; complete corresponding Chapter Activities (pages 8-13).
- Play Tic Tac Word (page 14).

Lesson II
- Continue with reading pages and Chapter Activities.
- Sequence the Site Flow Chart (page 19).
- Choose a Creative Writing Topic (page 22).
- Complete Site Map (page 25).

Lesson III
- Continue with reading pages and Chapter Activities.
- Work out Archaeology Word problems (page 23).
- Make pottery (page 21).
- Classify words (page 20).

Lesson IV
- Continue with reading pages and Chapter Activities.
- Do some science simulations (page 24).
- Simulate cave drawings (page 21).
- Research archaeologists (page 16).

Lesson V
- Do a comprehension check (page 26).
- Learn about animals of prehistory (page 27).
- Write a class newspaper as a culminating activity (#4, page 7).
- Learn about experts on a dig (page 28).

Overview of Activities

SETTING THE STAGE

1. **Archaeology.** Set up an archaeology center in your classroom. Gather resources—including textbooks, trade books, magazines, maps, and atlases—to display at this center. For some suggested titles see Etc., page 77, and the bibliography on page 80.

2. **Define archaeology.** Brainstorm with the whole class. Write the word archaeology on the board and tell students to write a definition of the term on an index card. Have them tape the card to a corner of their desk and save it for a future assignment. After the text has been read, direct them to again write a definition of archaeology. Compare the original definition with the new one. Discuss how the initial definition may have changed.

3. **Bulletin Board.** Begin a current events bulletin board of archaeological information. See page 75 for ideas on constructing this and other bulletin boards. Finding information could be a homework activity assigned to students on a rotating basis. Have students share their homework with the whole class or in small groups.

4. **Read a coin.** Group the students and supply each group with a penny or other coin. Challenge them to make a list of things they can learn about the people who made the coin just by examining it. Look on page 17 for a prepared lesson. A related activity is the artifact box project found on page 16.

5. **Read aloud.** Introduce the topic of archaeology with a book excerpt. Read aloud to students a section from *Canyons Beyond the Sky* by Laurence Kittleman (Atheneum, 1985) or the Newbery award-winner, *The Story of Mankind*, by Hendrick Willem Van Loon (Liveright, 1985). See the bibliography on page 80 for additional titles.

ENJOYING THE BOOK

1. **Chapter Activities.** Assign a number of pages for daily reading and the corresponding Chapter Activities (pages 8 to 13). Other plans for determining how you will employ the pages of *The Usborne Young Scientist: Archaeology* can be seen on page 15, Using the Pages.

2. **Flow Chart.** After the students have read about a dig site and the process involved in excavating the land, check their comprehension with the flow chart on page 19. If you prefer, copy the sentences on the chalkboard or overhead projector. Call on a student to come to the board and write the first step. That student in turn can choose the next participant; continue in this manner until all steps have been listed correctly.

3. **A Site Map.** Improve number skills and spatial relationships with the sample site map on page 25.

4. **Building Vocabulary.** In each section of the Chapter Activities, you will find a list of suggested vocabulary words from the text. Reinforce these and other words with the games on page 14. Expand critical thinking with the Word Classification activity (page 20) where students will categorize words.

Overview of Activities *(cont.)*

ENJOYING THE BOOK *(cont.)*

5. **Archaeological Art.** Although pottery is one of the most plentiful artifacts, a whole pot is a rarity. Students can make pots the old-fashioned coil way by following the directions on page 21. On that same page are directions for cave drawings, another kind of artifact that would be fun for students to duplicate.

6. **Writing Topics.** Page 22 describes four different ways to incorporate creative writing into the archaeology unit. Also included on the same page are twelve suggested topics that will tap into the creativity and imagination of your class.

$$\Box \quad P = 4\ell$$
$$A = \ell^2$$

7. **Archaeology Word Problems.** Learn more or review concepts about square measurement with the math word problems on page 23.

8. **Simulations.** Explore science concepts with the two experiments on page 24. These can be conducted in small groups or as a whole class demonstration.

EXTENDING THE BOOK

1. **Early Achievements.** To check students' understanding and comprehension of early humankind, assign pairs to complete the checklist on page 26. Follow up by assigning written reports on each of the four groupings listed. Include information about significant achievements, a description of daily life, clothing, food, housing, and physical characteristics.

2. **Animals of Prehistory.** After completing the wordsearch puzzle on page 27, students will have a list of some of the animals alive at the time of prehistoric humans. Make a class mural of these creatures. Tape a long sheet of gray or white butcher paper to the wall. Encourage students to use chalk or paints to complete their drawings.

3. **Read Some Other Usborne Books.** This company publishes many books related to archaeology, including *The First Civilisations* by Dr. Anne Millard (1977), *Living in Prehistoric Times* by Jane Chisholm (1982), and *The Children's Picture Prehistory: Early Man* by Jane Chisholm (1982).

4. **Putting It All Together.** Culminate this section with a class writing project—a newspaper. Title it *Prehistoric Times* or *News of the Early Years* or other appropriate name. In this project students will be able to synthesize their knowledge in a fun group activity. For information and help in writing a class newspaper see Teacher Created Materials' book #137 *Newspaper Reporters*.

5. **Dig Experts.** Learn about all the Experts on a Dig. Use the worksheet on page 28.

Chapter Activities

The Usborne Young Scientist: Archaeology can be utilized in a variety of ways. Some methods will be explored on this and the following five pages. Keep in mind that these are only suggestions; activities should be changed and adapted to fit your classroom program. Ideas for reinforcing the listed vocabulary words are presented on page 15. Note: If it is not feasible to provide every student with a copy of this suggested text, consider purchasing one book for each group of students. An alternate idea is to purchase one or two copies for your reference library; assign times for student pairs or groups to use the book.

Pre-reading Activity: Before students begin reading this book, conduct a brainstorming session to define the term *archaeology.* Record all responses on chart paper, the chalkboard, or the overhead projector. Save the responses to compare with the definition provided in the text. An alternative activity can be found on page 6, #2 under Setting the Stage. Other introductory methods for you to choose from are discussed on page 16.

Detectives of the Past

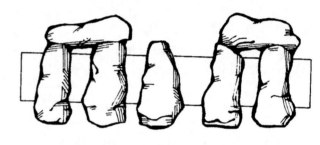

* Research and learn more about any of the following: Stonehenge; other archaeologists and their accomplishments (See page 69 for more information.); Mesopotamia and the city of Ur (See pages 45 to 53.); computer programs. (See Etc., page 77.)

* Begin a current events bulletin board (See page 75 for more ideas.); have the students add to it regularly.

* Make time capsules. Assign groups and direct them to make a list of artifacts that they think should be included in a time capsule. Check to see that the objects reflect their current lifestyles before placing them in a capsule. To make a time capsule, cut a soda bottle in half along the circumference, add the items desired, and tape the bottle together with duct tape or library tape. (Custom-designed time capsule kits can be purchased through Tom Snyder Productions, Inc., 80 Coolidge Hill Road, Watertown, MA, 02172-2817; phone 1-800-342-0236.)

* Vocabulary: archaeology, archaeologist, analysis, inscriptions, complex, calculations, technology, honored, analyze, civilizations.

Clues from the Past

* Pair the students to work together in creating a chart that explains the various ways that clues from the past are destroyed.

* Assign the students to write a paragraph explaining how natural forces destroy evidence of the past.

Chapter Activities *(cont.)*

Clues from the Past *(cont.)*

* Some clues from the past have been preserved. Have the students fold a sheet of drawing paper into fourths. In each section tell them to draw a picture of a clue which has been preserved. Below each picture write two or three sentences explaining how that item was preserved.

* Vocabulary: processes, fanatics, conquistadors, neighboring, bacteria, fungi, resins, mummification, silica, calcium, ritual, sarcophagus, peat bogs, tannic acid, meter.

Looking for Evidence

* For homework instruct the students to look for evidences of the past; have them sketch drawings of their findings or write descriptions of what they have found. Share the findings in small groups.

* Aerial photographs reveal clues that may not be readily recognized or seen at ground level. Examine some pictures that display a bird's-eye view. Have the students draw a picture of something from an aerial view—for example, the landscape as seen from the window of an airplane or tall building.

* Some clues are found because of their magnetic field. With students use a metal detector in an area which is not currently protected by law or being excavated for archaeological purposes. See what treasures can be found. You may want to salt the area ahead of time with coins and other metal objects that can easily be detected.

* Vocabulary: aerial, plowing, kiln, color, resistivity surveying, proton magnetometer, labyrinth, galleon, sonar, infrared.

Digging into the Past

* Group the students and have each group construct a flow chart that shows the step-by-step process of planning and carrying out an actual dig. Follow up with the worksheet on page 19.

* Students will need unlined index cards or other heavy paper and colored pencils or thin-lined marking pens for this activity. Direct the students to draw a picture and write a description on each index card of a tool or piece of equipment used by archaeologists and geologists on a site.

* Found objects are classified according to material. Provide students with some classifying practice. Prepare an object bag for each assigned group by placing a variety of small metal objects (nuts and bolts, nails, coins, paper clips, etc.), fabrics (material remnants, felt, yarn, ribbon, etc.), and bones (dried chicken or fish bones, seashells, clam shells, etc.) in a paper bag. Give one bag to each group and instruct them to classify the objects. Have students share their classifications with the whole group. The worksheet on page 20 can be used in conjunction with this activity.

* Vocabulary: excavation, site, stratified, burrowing, sieve, theodolite, rescue dig, salvage, industrial, gradually.

Chapter Activities *(cont.)*

The Underwater Detectives

* Write the following quote on the board or overhead projector; tell the students to write a one- or two-paragraph explanation.

  "An underwater dig may be up to 25 times as expensive as a land dig, and it is difficult for archaeologists to raise enough money for the latest equipment."

* Have students explain in their own words how Henry VIII's flagship, *Mary Rose*, was finally raised to the surface. Or have them explain how air-filled bags are used to lift heavy objects. Students can perform their own heavy-lifting experiment with the activity on page 24.

* Read some books about underwater explorations. Two recommended titles follow: *Diving to the Past* by W. John Hackwell (Charles Scribner's Sons, 1988) and *Undersea Archaeology* by Christopher Lampton (Franklin Watts, 1988).

* Vocabulary: communicate, survey, sonic, silt, monitor, aqualungs, trowels, concretions, amphorae, harbor, winches, fjord, incense.

Piecing the Evidence Together

* Archaeologists use all the artifacts they have found to put together an overall view of how the people of a particular time and/or culture lived. Have students simulate this method by examining and reading the contents of a wastebasket. Go to the school cafeteria for a sample basket or bring one of your own from home. Dump the contents onto newspaper. Examine labels and food scraps to tell what kind of diet these people had. See if there is any evidence of their monetary system. Look for newspapers or flyers to give clues about the community.

* For homework, assign students to bring in a picture from their family photo album—the older the picture the better. In small groups discuss what the clothing, hair, and jewelry of those pictured tells about the times. Pictures from old magazines or books may be substituted for family photos.

* Draw some cave art. See page 21 for complete instructions.

* Vocabulary: phasing, economic, courtiers, mosaic, lute, lyre, ornament, ancestor, status, hostile, embedded, enamel, ceremonial.

Pottery

* Make clay pots. On page 21 you will find directions for creating a pot using the coil method. A recipe for clay is also included.

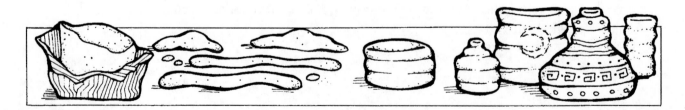

Chapter Activities *(cont.)*

Pottery *(cont.)*

* Pottery tells archaeologists much about the customs and daily life of the people. Pair the students and have them write a list of some of the things pottery tells us about others, or have them make a list of all the possible uses for pots.

* Tell the students to choose an age or assign a different age to each pair or group. Have them research pots of that particular time period. Direct them to notice especially the scenes engraved or painted on the sides of the pots. Instruct them to draw a pot with scenes that reflect the time period they were assigned. Display all work.

* Vocabulary: kiln, Mesopotamia, sherds, corpus, extracting, pithos, rituals, urns, Munsell Soil Color Chart.

Burials and Bodies

* Before assigning these two pages, brainstorm with the students all the information they think can be obtained from skeletons and graves. Record all responses on the chalkboard or overhead projector and save. Read the pages; re-examine the list and add more responses to it.

* As a class, discuss the health of ancient Egyptians. Ask students whether or not they think the Egyptians were a healthy people. Tell them to defend their statements with evidence from the text.

* Many ancient cultures buried their dead with things they thought would be needed in the next life. Tell students to list some of the items found buried with the bodies.

* Vocabulary: arthritis, spectrometry, unravel, inscription, seeped, chieftain, perished, canopic jars, natron, pagan.

Animal and Plant Remains

* Discuss how plant remains can indicate what the climate was like in the past, how archaeologists can tell what kind of animals lived in an area, and how archaeologists can determine the environment from plant remains.

* Examine grains of pollen under a microscope. Instruct the students to draw pictures of these magnified samples.

* The Native Americans of North America were more efficient hunters than the European settlers because they hunted for deer of all ages. What other reasons might explain why the Europeans fared so poorly when it came to hunting?

* Vocabulary: efficient, domesticated, descendant, mature, peat bogs, species, flotation, hollyhocks, garland.

Chapter Activities *(cont.)*

Buildings, Writing

* Build a model of one of the ancient homes pictured in the text. Use toothpicks, wood craft sticks, plaster of Paris, clay, homemade dough, cardboard, twigs, or other materials to complete the project. Assign pairs or groups of students to work on a building. Tell them to make a label for their building which explains some of the history of the architecture. Display the completed models for all to view.

* Read another text to find out more about ancient buildings. Two recommended titles are *Going on a Dig* by Velma Ford Morrison (Dodd , Mead & Company, 1981) and *Prehistory* by Keith Branigan (Warwick Press, 1984).

* Remnants of Greek and Latin can still be found in the English language today. Instruct the students to make a list of twenty English words that have a Greek or a Latin prefix or suffix. They should be able to explain what each means.

* Research the Sumerians and the invention of writing. Find out about the pictographs they first used and their evolution into cuneiform. Have students devise their own cuneiform letters.

* Vocabulary: wattle and daub, architect, inscriptions, dedication, cuneiform, demolished, ziggurat, aqueduct, elaborate, resemble, pulverize, glyphs, hieroglyphs.

How Old Is It?

* Group the students and have each group make a chart which shows the dating techniques that archaeologists use. Illustrations should be included along with the text.

* If possible, find a tree stump and try to figure out the age of the tree by counting its growth rings. Follow the recommendations in the text.

* Why isn't it possible to work out one master tree ring pattern for the whole world? Research bristlecone pines in America to find out where they grow best and how old they are.

* Vocabulary: potassium, argon, fission, radioactive, collagen, radiocarbon, organic, papyrus, dendrochronology, fluorine.

Radioactive Dating

* "Carbon 14 dating caused a revolution when it was first used in the 1950s..." Tell why and explain how the process works.

* What does the prefix *thermo* in the word *thermoluminescence* mean? Define the word *thermoluminescence.* Write a list of five other words that begin with or contain *thermo;* define each word.

* Discuss with students which dating method is the most important and useful. Or is one technique better than another? Talk about the pros and cons of each.

* Vocabulary: half-life, contaminated, inclusion, detect, cosmic, photosynthesis, obsidian, fission, thermoluminescence.

Chapter Activities *(cont.)*

Preserving the Past

* To demonstrate how to protect wood from decay, try this experiment. You will need two wood boards, a paintbrush, and some weather-protective coating (available at a hardware store). Prepare one board with the protective coating and allow ample time to dry. Place both boards outside in a spot where they will get plenty of sun. Pour the same amount of water over both boards every day. Observe what happens to the wood over a period of at least two weeks.

* Find a large picture of a pottery object and copy it on a copy machine. Glue the picture to a cardboard background and allow to dry. Cut the picture into a number of jigsaw pieces and place all of them in a manila envelope. Trade puzzles with a friend and solve them.

* Design and draw a helmet for a king from ancient times or make a scale model of one from clay or homemade clay. (For recipe, see page 21.) Embed objects in the clay to make the helmet look authentic.

* Vocabulary: conservation, biological, processes, conservators, vacuum, garnets, genuine, molds, neutrons, activation.

Putting Theories to the Test

* With the students, discuss why archaeologists make copies of the buildings, pots, tools, and weapons of ancient times. Talk about what archaeologists can learn from these re-creations.

* Make a crude tool from craft sticks or wooden ice cream sticks. Rub one end of the stick on an angle over a sidewalk or other rough surface; rub the opposite side of the stick in the same manner to form a V. Use to make carvings or engravings in pottery and other clay artifacts.

* Sample a variety of grains such as wheat, bran, barley, bulgur wheat, etc. All can be found at a health food store. Construct a class graph to show which grains the students liked best and least.

* Vocabulary: flint, similar, porridge, ballista, thatched, descendant.

The Uses of Pottery to the Archaeologist

* Bring in some pots for students to observe. Tell students to look at the checklist on page 30 of the text and answer the questions based on their observations of the pots. Write a description of one of the pots, using the same format as shown on that page.

* Vocabulary: decay, glean, mould, unglazed, burnished, glazed.

Archaeological Vocabulary

Throughout this archaeology unit you will encounter vocabulary words which you will want to introduce and reinforce. Some fun, motivating methods are described below. Modify them where necessary to suit your classroom needs.

Tic-Tac-Word

strata	sieve	mosaic
fungi	silt	lute
urns	lyre	sherds

This is played just like the familiar tic-tac-toe game, but it does have a twist. On the chalkboard or overhead projector, draw a tic-tac-toe grid. In each square write a different vocabulary word. Divide the class into two teams. Determine which team goes first; call it the X team. Call on the first person of the X team to define any word on the tic-tac-toe board. If the response is correct, the team gets an X in that square, but if the response is incorrect, an O goes in the square. Now it is the first player on the O team to choose a word. Scoring proceeds in the same manner as described. A game is won when a team has three in a row. At the end of each game, erase the words and add new ones. Play begins where it left off on the previous game. Best three out of five games wins the championship for the day.

Variation: After the students are familiar with this game, let them pair up to challenge another pair. They may prepare their own tic-tac-toe boards complete with vocabulary words.

Quick Quiz

For a quick review use this method. Write the list of vocabulary words on the chalkboard or overhead projector. Call on a student to define any word of his/her choosing. That student, in turn, chooses another person to use the word in a sentence so that the definition of the word is clear. Go on to the next word for a definition and a sentence; continue to let students choose the next respondent.

Dig for Words

Divide the students into small groups or pairs to work together on this project. Have each group choose one person to act as the secretary.

Write a multi-syllablic word on the chalkboard or overhead projector. Direct the students to copy it vertically on a sheet of paper. After each letter of the word, write one or two words that begin or end with that letter and that also pertain to the topic of archaeology. For example, if the word *artifact* were chosen, *archaeology* or *bolla* could be written on the first line. (See diagram.) After a predetermined time limit, share the completed lists with the whole class.

```
archaeology
r
t
i
f
       a
boll   c
       t
```

Foreign Spellings

Throughout the text of *The Usborne Young Scientist: Archaeology,* you and your students may notice that some words are spelled differently than they usually are. Ask students to speculate on some possible reasons. (The book is printed in London, England, and some of their spellings vary from ours.) As these words are read in the text, add them to an ongoing list of foreign spellings and compare them to regular usage. (These words include *honoured, plough, mould, colour, analyse, harbour,* etc.)

Using the Pages

On this page you will find a number of ideas for implementing *The Usborne Young Scientist: Archaeology* text in your classroom. Change and adapt these ideas as you need and invent some of your own, too.

* **Archaeology Center.** Set up an archaeology center within the room. Stock it with numerous reference materials including textbooks, trade books, magazines, maps, and atlases. See the bibliography on page 80 and also see Etc., page 77, for a list of some suggested titles.

  Keep one or two copies of *The Usborne Young Scientist: Archaeology* at the center. Make copies of the Chapter Activities on pages 8 to 13 and laminate them. Punch holes along one side of the pages with a three-hole punch. Attach hole reinforcers on each hole, both back and front. Insert the pages in a plastic-covered three-ring binder. Assign pairs or groups to work on the pages during a specified time on a rotating basis.

* **Topics.** Divide the book into five or six topic areas, (e.g., How Artifacts Are Preserved, or Conducting a Dig). Give students only those activities from pages 8 to 13 that pertain to their assigned topic. For example, activities to accompany the subject of conducting a dig can be found on page 9. A prepared worksheet is also included on page 19.

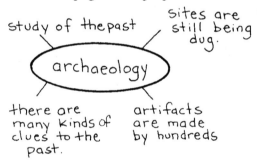

* **Webbing.** With the whole class, construct a web of what students know about archaeology and what they would like to learn. Have each pair or group choose a different idea from the web that they would like to know more about. *The Usborne Young Scientist: Archaeology* book can be used as a reference resource along with other books you have available. Encourage library research for more in-depth reporting on a topic.

* **Chapters.** Assign one chapter each day to a different group. Have them use this textbook to complete the appropriate activities for that chapter. The next day a different group is assigned another chapter. When all the chapters have been covered the students can share their projects with the whole class. (Delete any, if necessary) Collate all written materials in a three-ring binder for a class archaeology book.

* **Workbook.** Make four or five copies of each of the workbook pages in this section. Laminate them and staple each to the inside of a separate file folder; label the outside of the folder with the title of the work page. Place all the folders at your archaeology center along with some water-based, wipe-off pens. Students can write on the laminated surface and then erase their answers when their work has been checked.

Introductory Methods

There are any number of ways to introduce a unit of study about archaeology. A few are outlined below. Choose the method that best fits your teaching style; modify any of the activities to fit your classroom needs.

1. **Read a Coin.** Give each group of students a coin (penny, nickel, etc.). Challenge the groups to make a list of things they can learn from the people who made the coin just by carefully examining it. A prepared coin reading activity can be found on page 17.

2. **At the Movies.** Preview first and decide to view all, or a selected part, of an Indiana Jones movie. (*Raiders of the Lost Ark* and its sequels are readily available at video stores nationwide.) Also, check with your school district media center to see which titles of *National Geographic* archaeology-related specials they may have.

3. **Artifact Boxes.** Make one artifact-filled shoebox for each group of students. Items to use could include small articles of clothing such as a sock or a glove, a ceramic figurine or statue, plastic utensils or cups, metal keys or tools, wooden spoons or clothespins, a can opener or other small kitchen utensil, pens or pencils, etc. Vary the articles among the boxes. Tell students to identify each object in their group's artifact box. Have them construct a chart that lists each item, its description, and some possible uses for that item. (See the sample work sheet on page 18.) Ask students to explain what the artifacts tell about the culture. Share their speculations in class.

4. **Read Aloud.** Read aloud to the students an appropriate selection from a periodical such as *Calliope,* a history magazine for young people. (The May/June 1992 issue is all about vanished civilizations. For more information on other journals to employ, see page 77.) After reading the article, have students discuss their impressions and address any questions they may have.

5. **Research.** Assign small groups of students to find out about past archaeologists. Direct each group to write the archaeolgist's most noted achievement. Some possible names to explore are British archaeologists Howard Carter, Dame Kathleen Kenyon, Sir A. Henry Layard, Sir W.M. Flinder Petrie, Sir R.E. Mortimer Wheeler, and Sir C. Leonard Woolley; Frenchman, Auguste Mariette; German, Heinrich Schliemann; Kenyans, Louis S.B. Leakey and his wife Mary Douglas Leakey; American Hiram Bingham. Follow up with a quiz matching archaeologists to their accomplishments. (See page 69.)

Heinrich Schliemann

6. **Discuss finding treasures, particularly ancient ones.** Bury small objects in a plastic swimming pool filled with sand; conduct a "dig."

Reading a Coin

This group activity is a great way to introduce the topic of archaeology and to motivate your students to learn more about the subject. First, divide the students into groups of three or four. Second, supply each group with a Lincoln penny. Third, give each group a copy of the questions below or assign a secretary in each group to copy the questions. (You can write them on the chalkboard or prepare an overhead transparency of the list.)

As a group, determine the answers to these questions by carefully examining the penny.

1. How old is the coin?
2. What languages are found on the coin?
3. What foreign phrase is on the coin?
4. Of what material is the coin made?
5. Name the person depicted on the coin.
6. What building is on the opposite side of the coin?
7. In which country was the coin made?
8. What is this coin used for?
9. Do you think these people are religious? Support your answer.
10. What is the monetary value of the coin?

After the groups have completed their examination of the penny, discuss the answers with the whole class. (Sample answers have been supplied for you in the box below.) Establish that the coin is an example of an artifact and that an artifact is any object made by humans. As a group, brainstorm some things that are artifacts; record the list on chart paper, the chalkboard, or overhead projector. Save for later use in writing reports, creative writing assignments, or other projects.

Answers to the coin questions above.

1. Answers will vary. To find the correct answer, subtract this year from the year imprinted on the penny.
2. English and Latin.
3. "E Pluribus Unum" which means "one out of many."
4. Metal including copper.
5. Abraham Lincoln.
6. The Lincoln Memorial in Washington, D.C.
7. United States of America.
8. It is used to buy things.
9. Yes, because the phrase "IN GOD WE TRUST" appears above Lincoln's head.
10. One cent or one-hundredth of a dollar.

Artifact Boxes

In the first column below, list the name of each artifact in your group's box. Use the space in the second column to write a description of the object. Write the use(s) of the object in the last column. At the bottom of the page write an explanation of what you think these artifacts tell about the culture of these people.

Artifact	Description	Possible Uses

This is what the artifacts tell about the culture of these people:

_____

_____

_____

_____

Site Flow Chart

Work on a dig is conducted in a methodical, organized manner. Certain steps have to be completed in order. Ten planning steps for a dig are listed in the box below. Write them in the correct order on the flow chart provided.

> * Place each find in a separate container according to its layer. *Use all the artifacts gathered to build up a picture of the people who once inhabited the site. *Examine the site for its size and types of soil and rocks. * Wash and dry the pottery. *Look for pottery, stones, or flints that might indicate the best place to start the digging. * At day's end, collect all finds together in one place. *Determine the number of workers and type of equipment that will be needed. *Mark each piece to indicate the site, the year, and the layer in which it was found. *Choose the site and consult landowners (if any). *Survey and draw up an accurate plan of the site.

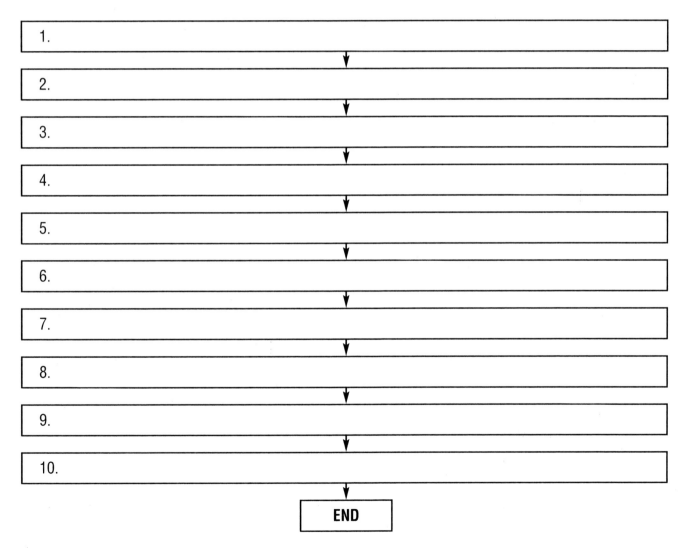

1.

2.

3.

4.

5.

6.

7.

8.

9.

10.

END

Word Classification

Just as archaeologists classify artifacts according to the material they are made of, you can classify words according to their make-up. In the box below you will find a list of archaeology-related words. Use them to write an answer to the questions that follow. Each word will be used only once.

ziggurat	mosaic	sonic helmet	silt	lute
sherds	cuneiform	sieve	volcanoes	mummification
aqueduct	chemicals	bacteria	lyre	fungi
urns	aqualung	peat bogs	carbon-14	hieroglyphs
trowel	pollution	theodolite	potassium-argon	
pictograph	strata	thermoluminescence	dendrochronology	

1. Which words name instruments you can play? _____

    _____

2. Which words have something to do with the soil?_____

    _____

3. Which words name structures?_____

    _____

4. Which words name forms of writing? _____

    _____

5. Which words name artifacts but not buildings? _____

    _____

6. Which words name things which destroy evidences of the past? _____

    _____

7. Which words are tools used at a dig? _____

    _____

8. Which words name things which preserve clues from the past? _____

9. Which words name things which date artifacts? _____

    _____

10. Which words name tools used in an underwater dig? _____

    _____

*Challenge:** Make up your own classification question using the words in the box above. See if you can stump your partner.

Archaeological Art

The art projects on this page can be incorporated into an archaeology unit wherever it is most appropriate. Both of them are related to some aspect of archaeology; possible tie-ins are provided at the beginning of each project.

Pottery. A whole, intact pot is a rare find for an archaeologist. Most of the time only broken pieces are found. Patterns and drawings on the pots help determine the period of the piece. Have students choose a time period that they would like to represent. Tell them to research and find pictures of pots from that era. Then have them make their own clay pot, bowl, or pitcher using the method that follows. Students may use commericial clay or make their own. (See the clay recipe below.)

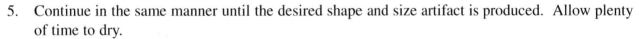
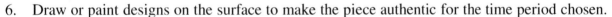

1. Shape the bottom of the vessel by flattening a ball of clay into the desired shape and size.
2. Roll clay into long snakes about one-fourth inch (.6 cm) to one half-inch (1.3 cm) thick.
3. Coil one clay snake around the base smoothing the coil onto the base with your fingers.
4. Place another coil on top of the previous layer; smooth into the first layer both inside and out.
5. Continue in the same manner until the desired shape and size artifact is produced. Allow plenty of time to dry.
6. Draw or paint designs on the surface to make the piece authentic for the time period chosen.

Clay Recipe: Mix four cups (944 mL) of salt with one cup (236 mL) of cornstarch in a pan. Add enough water to form a paste. Cook over medium heat, stirring constantly. When the water is evaporated, remove from the stove and allow to cool.

Cave Drawings. Some 30,000 years ago, early humans used charcoal to draw pictures on the inside walls of caves. Stalactite formations that wrinkled the surface of the rock were incorporated into the drawings. Students can simulate their own cave drawings with this project. Materials needed are flour, salt, water, black tempera paint, plastic squeeze bottles, measuring cup, cardboard, gray paint, paintbrush, and pencil.

1. Prepare the surface of the cardboard with the gray paint; allow to dry.
2. Mix equal parts of the flour, salt, and water; add some black tempera paint and mix well.
3. Pour the mixture into the squeeze bottles and attach the lids tightly.
4. With the pencil, lightly draw the outline of an animal or human as the cave dweller might have drawn it.
5. Squeeze the black paint over the pencil-drawn lines. When dry, the black outline should glisten to resemble the chalk on the stalactites of a cave.

Alternate Method: Have the students use black chalk or a piece of charcoal to draw appropriate designs on gray construction paper.

Writing Topics

This page can be utilized in a variety of ways. Some suggestions follow:

* Assign a different topic each day; give students a choice of topics.

* Make this topic list available to each group of students. Allow them to choose their own project to complete together.

* Cut apart the topics on the lines and put them into a lunch bag or a box. Have each student draw one.

* Number each topic. Tell students to count off from one to twelve. (Repeat when twelve is reached.) Students must write on the subject that matches their number.

---

1. Write step-by-step directions telling how pottery is made or how you can make your own pottery. Illustrate each step.

2. Some ancient peoples are named after their pottery (e.g. the Beaker People.) Draw a picture of a pot and name some people after it.

3. Most ancient cultures buried their dead with items they thought would be necessary in the afterlife. What would you take with you in the afterlife and why?

4. Describe a toy that children from an ancient era might have played with. Include only those materials that were available at the time.

5. You have been assigned to construct a time capsule of your family. The container is no bigger than a shoe box. What objects will you put in it and why?

6. Develop an alphabet system of cuneiforms or pictographs. Write a secret message with it and give it to a partner to translate.

7. What qualities do you think are necessary to become an archaeologist? How many of those same qualities do you have?

8. Some ancient writings have yet to be decoded. However, you think you have found the secret to translating an old Mayan astronomy book. Write one page of text and its translation.

9. You have volunteered to work on a new dig in a foreign country. Keep a diary account for one week of your exploits and adventures.

10. Invent a new machine that can find currently undetectable artifacts. Draw and label a picture of your invention; tell how it works.

11. One of your friends has found an ancient statue. He wants to keep it and sell it. You think it should be turned over to a local museum. Convince your friend that you are right.

12. Write a story about the daily life of a person your age in ancient Mesopotamia or other prehistoric age.

Archaeological Word Problems

Read each word problem below and solve; show your work in the space provided.

1. Professor Digg decided to use 5 meter by 5 meter squares at the dig site. What is the area of one square?

2. At another dig site, squares were 6 feet by 6 feet and 3 feet deep. What is the volume of one square?

3. Squares at an old site are 36 inches by 36 inches. What is the perimeter of one square in inches? in feet?

4. The professor measured a 20m by 30m area. How many square meters is that?

5. Within one square, a trench 6 feet long, 2 feet wide, and 2 feet deep was cut. What is the volume of the trench?

6. The area of one dig site is 121 square meters. What is the length of one side?

7. If the squares at Professor Digg's site are 81 square inches in area, what are the dimensions of each side?

8. At a new site squares are 200 cm per side. What is the perimeter in meters of each square?

Challenge: Write your own word problem. Show it to a partner and have him/her solve it.

Science Connections

These simulations will help students understand some important science concepts. Experiments can be done within groups or as a demonstration for the whole class.

Underwater Archaeology

Air-filled bags are used to lift heavy objects underwater. The principle behind this can be demonstrated with a balloon and a large book.

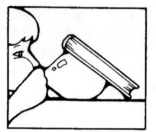

* Place the book on a table so that its spine is flush with the edge of the table. (See diagram.)
* Lift the book and place the balloon underneath it, so that the neck of the balloon hangs over the edge.
* Blow up the balloon and watch the book rise.

To demonstrate this principle underwater, you will need one small balloon, a small paperweight or rock, duct tape, and a large container of water such as an aquarium.

* Securely attach the paperweight to the balloon with the tape.
* Inflate the balloon and pinch the neck closed.
* With one hand, bring the balloon and paperweight to the bottom of the water. Let go of the neck and watch what happens.

Sound Through Water

Underwater archaeologists use sonic helmets to communicate under water. To establish that sound does indeed travel through water, demonstrate with this simple experiment. You will need a mug of water, a metal spoon, and a straw.

* Pair the students for this exercise.
* One partner taps the outside of the mug with the spoon; listen to the pitch of the sound.
* Now have one partner blow bubbles with the straw into the mug of water while the other partner taps the outside of the mug with the spoon. Notice the change in pitch.

Have the students try this one on their own with a partner. Tell them to go swimming with a buddy. They will need two metal spoons or two rocks. One partner stays with his/her head above the water while the other person taps the spoons or rocks under the water. What do they hear? On the next try, the partner puts his/her head under the water, while the other person taps the spoons or rocks underwater. Now do they hear anything? Have volunteers report their findings to the class.

* To learn more about underwater archaeology, read *Diving to the Past* by W. John Hackwell (Charles Scribner's Sons, 1988) or *Undersea Archaeology* by Christopher Lampton (Franklin Watts, 1988).

A Site Map

Below is a sample site map. Note how it is divided into four sections or quadrants—northeast, northwest, southeast, and southwest. Also note that each square is numbered. Study the number patterns in the northeast and the northwest quadrants. Supply the missing numbers in the southeast and southwest sections by writing the correct numbers in the circles.

NW   **N**   **NE**

Grid (north of the W–E axis):

						28	23						
				27	21	16	24						
			26	20	15	11	17	25					
		25	19	14	10	7	12	18	26				
	24	18	13	9	6	4	8	13	19	27			
23	17	12	8	5	3	2	5	9	14	20	28		
22	16	11	7	4	2	1	1	3	6	10	15	21	29

W ←————————————————————→ **E**

Grid (south of the W–E axis; ◯ = circle to be filled in):

		15	10	◯	3	1	◯	◯	4	◯	11	◯	22
	28	20	14	◯	5	◯	3	◯	8	◯	17	23	
	◯	◯	◯	◯	◯	◯		9	13	◯	24		
		◯	18	12	7	◯	14	19	25				
			◯	◯	◯	◯	20	◯					
				24	16	◯	◯						
					23	◯							

SW   **S**   **SE**

Early Achievements

Humans developed some considerable advances from the time of Homo habilis some 2,500,000 years ago to the age of the Cro-Magnon 40,000 years ago.

Read each statement below. Fill in the circle(s) of those humans who achieved that development.

	Homo habilis	Homo erectus	Homo sapiens (Neanderthal)	Homo sapiens (Cro-Magnon)
1. Made fire 70,000 years ago	○	○	○	○
2. First used crude stone tools 2,500,000 years ago	○	○	○	○
3. First evidences of art 30,000 years ago	○	○	○	○
4. Planned burials 50,000 years ago	○	○	○	○
5. Made bone harpoons 30,000 years ago	○	○	○	○
6. Were able to control fire 400,000 years ago	○	○	○	○
7. Showed no evidences of art	○	○	○	○
8. Fired clay 27,000 years ago	○	○	○	○
9. Constructed a hand-axe 1,500,000 years ago	○	○	○	○
10. Displayed no evidence of burial rites	○	○	○	○

Animals of Prehistory

Prehistoric animals thrived during the time of prehistoric humans, but the dinosaur did not. Those monstrous species existed millions of years before the arrival of humans, who arrived too late to view the giant creatures. There were, however, a number of animals around during the ascent of humans. Eighteen of them are named in the wordsearch below. Find all eighteen and list them on the spaces provided below the wordsearch puzzle. Words may be up, down, backwards, or diagonal.

```
U  S  E  L  T  C  B  D  S  T  E  A  P  E  E  H  S  E  G  N  N  M  M  F  H  B  N  H
A  P  S  I  H  H  O  I  N  E  N  E  E  W  N  L  I  T  O  O  S  W  I  R  I  E  O  I
B  A  I  N  I  I  I  B  E  X  S  S  Y  O  G  E  S  I  O  N  T  I  S  I  S  C  T  M
O  C  A  G  S  W  N  C  F  E  A  C  O  D  I  B  L  H  I  F  E  L  T  Z  B  A  R  Y
N  E  M  U  M  A  E  E  O  N  J  R  U  O  N  I  A  I  N  O  R  D  E  E  E  U  E  N
S  E  V  L  O  P  S  H  S  H  E  I  E  G  G  T  T  S  G  S  C  B  E  N  S  G  I  P
V  S  R  A  E  R  S  O  T  I  E  B  S  R  T  M  L  W  T  S  R  O  R  D  S  S  A  A
O  O  U  L  S  E  E  L  U  P  N  I  T  D  H  O  E  O  O  A  A  A  N  A  A  E  L  M
Y  I  N  M  S  T  D  A  M  P  E  R  A  S  A  R  A  R  S  U  L  R  F  N  G  I  L  E
M  U  S  K  O  X  I  E  S  O  S  P  R  H  I  N  O  C  E  R  O  S  O  D  E  A  Y  A
A  M  N  E  A  T  C  G  A  T  P  A  V  E  N  E  S  D  D  M  I  I  S  C  T  M  N  I
G  U  I  S  G  Y  E  I  B  A  A  R  E  A  T  T  N  A  H  P  E  L  E  O  O  T  S  S
E  S  N  S  E  G  A  R  E  M  N  T  Z  R  H  C  T  S  A  H  F  N  S  L  E  W  A  W
A  T  G  A  I  O  E  A  S  U  O  E  B  C  N  O  S  I  B  O  O  W  U  L  A  R  Y  E
D  B  O  G  S  E  S  F  C  S  L  D  Y  A  E  H  A  E  Y  W  R  E  O  L  N  I  M  L
I  I  U  E  D  O  I  F  O  I  Y  E  O  H  B  A  L  A  I  I  N  P  M  E  E  T  Y  T
O  D  T  N  A  D  K  E  M  N  P  M  V  I  L  O  I  R  H  S  E  S  O  A  Y  I  N  I
S  Y  I  Y  T  H  O  N  O  G  A  I  O  G  A  L  O  C  O  S  I  T  F  G  H  N  A  C
T  E  O  I  R  U  N  J  S  L  R  M  Y  A  S  L  T  N  P  I  A  M  T  U  M  G  M  A
R  O  F  K  I  H  I  A  E  E  K  L  E  V  T  E  T  H  S  T  S  I  C  E  Y  T  E  Y
```

1. _____   10. _____

2. _____   11. _____

3. _____   12. _____

4. _____   13. _____

5. _____   14. _____

6. _____   15. _____

7. _____   16. _____

8. _____   17. _____

9. _____   18. _____

Dig Experts

Archaeologists are not the only experts present on a dig. A team of people works together to gather as much information from the clues as possible. While some of these experts work in the field on a daily basis, others complete their work in science laboratories and museums. To find out more about some of these workers, fill in the blanks with the correct name. Use words from the Dig Expert Box at the bottom of the page.

1. The _____ has the difficult job of decoding ancient languages, many of which are no longer spoken or written. Inscriptions have to be decoded symbol by symbol.

2. By studying and identifying plants grown in the past, the _____ can tell the archaeologist about food sources and even the climate of a particular period.

3. Each day, the _____ draws newly found objects. This work is usually done on graph paper to help keep artifacts, and their relationships to each other, precisely to scale.

4. These scientists study rocks and minerals. _____ also study the way the land was formed. Their job is to find what kinds of rocks and minerals may have been available for building and tool-making.

5. Fossil remains of plants and animals are studied by _____. In addition to identifying and cataloging information, they theorize about how early plants and animals lived.

6. One job of the _____ is to reconstruct pots by piecing together broken sherds. This expert identifies pottery by shape and design, glaze, and chemical content of the clay.

7. The _____ works both on and off the site. The resulting pictures must show artifacts in their proper perspective. A meter stick is placed close to an object to show size accurately.

8. Identifying animal species and the ways they have evolved is the job of the _____. This specialist examines the many uses early people had for animals from clothing to shelter, to tools and weapons.

9. Artifacts must be carefully cataloged and stored so that objects can easily be found when needed for testing and identification. It is the responsibility of the _____ to keep meticulous records.

10. Physical characteristics of human beings are studied by the physical _____. Some of this scientist's duties include identifying human remains, particularly bones.

paleontologists	ceramist	artist	epigrapher	geologists
photographer	botanist	registrar	anthropologist	zoologist

Dig This! How Archaeologists Uncover Our Past

by Michael Avi-Yonah

Summary

In Dig This! How Archaeologists Uncover Our Past *the reader learns how the tombs and ruins of ancient cities and shipwrecks on the ocean floor have helped archaeologists uncover the secrets of these centuries-old cultures. Through the discovery of pottery, tools, weapons, and other artifacts, scientists have been able to piece together daily life in ancient times. While some of these explorations were carefully planned other sites were discovered by accident. The Lascaux Cave in France, for example, was unearthed by a group of boys exploring a forest. No matter how the sites were found, their clues are equally important. Civilizations of the Middle East and Asia, the Mediterranean, and the Americas are addressed in separate chapters in this text to give a global look at how humans have evolved on our planet.*

Sample Plan

Lesson I

- Map the ancient world (page 32).
- Take a vocabulary pre-test (page 33).
- Read Chapters 1 and 2.
- Complete a science activity — a model of the strata (page 34).
- Classify methods of dating artifacts (page 37).
- Begin using writing prompts from page 44.

Lesson II

- Read Chapter 3.
- Map the Ancient Civilizations of the Middle East and Asia (page 34).
- Construct a chart of changes in handwriting (page 34).
- Explore King Tut's Tomb (page 38).
- Continue writing prompts from page 44.

Lesson III

- Read Chapter 4.
- Map the Ancient Mediterranean (page 34).
- Compare the Minoans with the Mycenaeans (page 39) or read the article about Pompeii (page 41).
- Make a New Age Relief (page 40).

Lesson IV

- Read Chapter 5.
- Map Ancient Mesoamerica.
- Create Mayan jars (page 40).
- Continue writing prompts (page 44).

Lesson V

- Read Chapter 6.
- Chart the Holy Land through the Stone, Bronze, and Iron Ages (page 35).
- Make clay masks (page 40).
- Compare ancient civilizations (page 36).

Lesson VI

- Read Chapters 7 and 8.
- Test knowledge of early archaeologists (page 42).
- Sequence date a modern object (page 35).
- Complete some ancient math (page 43).
- Determine a class project (page 36).

Overview of Activities

SETTING THE STAGE

---

1. Read aloud a literature selection about ancient times. Many suitable pieces are available. See page 80 for some suggestions or use "Ulysses and the Cyclops" from the *Odyssey* by Homer (it is included in *Classics to Read Aloud to Your Children* by William F.Russell, 1984) or any tale from *D'Aulaires' Book of Greek Myths* by Ingri and Edgar Parin D'Aulaire (Dell Publishing, 1962). Discuss what role myths played in ancient life. Ask students how we know about these ancient myths.

2. Pair the students and give each pair a copy of the map on page 32. Instruct them to use research materials to help them label the map. Assign the students to write on the back of the paper five facts they have discovered in their research about each civilization listed on the map. Have them add their facts to a classroom chart.

3. Display a world map. Assign pairs or groups of students to find all the locations from the mapping exercise, #2, on the map. A globe may be substituted for the world map.

4. In a class discussion explore the role of archaeologists and the importance of their discoveries. Record student responses on chart paper and set aside. At the end of the unit, discuss again the role of archaeologists. Compare their later answers with their initial responses.

ENJOYING THE BOOK

---

1. Assess students' knowledge and understanding of the text's vocabulary with the exercise on page 33. This activity can be used as a pre and a post-test, if desired. Extend the activity. Instruct the students to find each word within the text of *Dig This! How Archaeologists Uncover Our Past* and copy the complete sentence in which each word appears.

2. Expand vocabulary skills with this project. Prepare a number of construction paper strips. With a marking pen, write a word on one side of a strip and its definition on the other. Make a strip for each vocabulary word. Student pairs can use the strips to quiz each other on meanings and spellings of the words.

3. On pages 34 to 36 you will find a number of related activities for each chapter. A variety of math, social studies, creative writing, geography, art, and critical thinking activities are provided from which to choose. Use those projects which best conform to your classroom needs. Modify them to suit your own teaching style.

4. On page 37 students can classify words and phrases related to the process of dating artifacts. Use the prepared chart or make a transparency of the page for use on an overhead projector.

5. Take a tour of King Tut's Tomb on page 38. Students will learn about the tomb's contents as they follow the directions. An excellent resource for this project is the book *Into the Mummy's Tomb* by Nicholas Reeves (Scholastic, Inc., 1992).

Overview of Activities *(cont.)*

Enjoying the Book *(cont.)*

---

6. Compare the ancient cultures of the Minoans and the Mycenaeans in a Venn diagram. See page 39. Pairs or individuals can be assigned to complete this page. As an alternative draw two intersecting circles on the chalkboard. Read aloud a clue and call on a student to write it in the proper section of the circles. Continue in this manner until all clues have been placed on the diagram.

7. Directions for three art projects are provided on page 40. Refer to the Across the Curriculum pages (pages 34 to 36) to find out to which chapters the art projects are directly related.

8. Have the students read the article about Pompeii on page 41. Assign different pairs or groups to complete the critical thinking activities that follow. Extend the lesson by researching more about Mt. Vesuvius and other volcanoes.

9. Let students take the multiple choice test on page 42 to find out how well they know their scientists. Make this an open-book test, if desired.

10. All the problems on page 43 are taken from information found in *Dig This! How Archaeologists Uncover Our Past.* Use the problems for homework or as a whole group lesson.

11. The writing topics on page 44 can be used throughout the unit as daily writing topics or as prompts for creative writing. Compile the stories into books for your classroom library.

Extending the Book

---

1. On page 35 you will find some ideas for a class project such as a letter-writing campaign or finding out about digs in your community. Let the students choose one or have them come up with an idea of their own.

2. Students can research some ancient civilizations and construct a chart. See page 36 for a sample. If preferred, make a class chart. Assign each group of students a particular civilization. Have them add their facts to a prepared class chart.

3. View an Indiana Jones movie. Rent one from a local video store or check with your school district and library for a copy. Preview the film before showing all or parts of it to the class. Discuss stereotypes about archaeologists with the class before and after the film. See page 36.

4. Go on a classroom dig. Complete directions and lessons can be found on pages 54 to 61.

5. Have these books on hand for students to use for research activities. The pictures, drawings, and text in each one will capture the attention of even the most reluctant reader.

Indiana Jones Explores Ancient Egypt by John Malam (Arcade Publishing, 1991)
The Kingfisher Book of the Ancient World by Hazel Mary Martel (Kingfisher, 1995)
The Visual Dictionary of Ancient Civilization edited by Emily Hill (Dorling Kindersley, 1994)

Mapping the Ancient World

The map below shows the sites of some of the world's first civilizations. Label the map with the following information: Egypt, Mesopotamia, Indian Ocean, Indus, China, Pacific Ocean, Mediterranean Sea, Crete, Africa, Mycenae, Roman Republic, Mesoamerica, Atlantic Ocean, and South America. Write the answer next to the number.

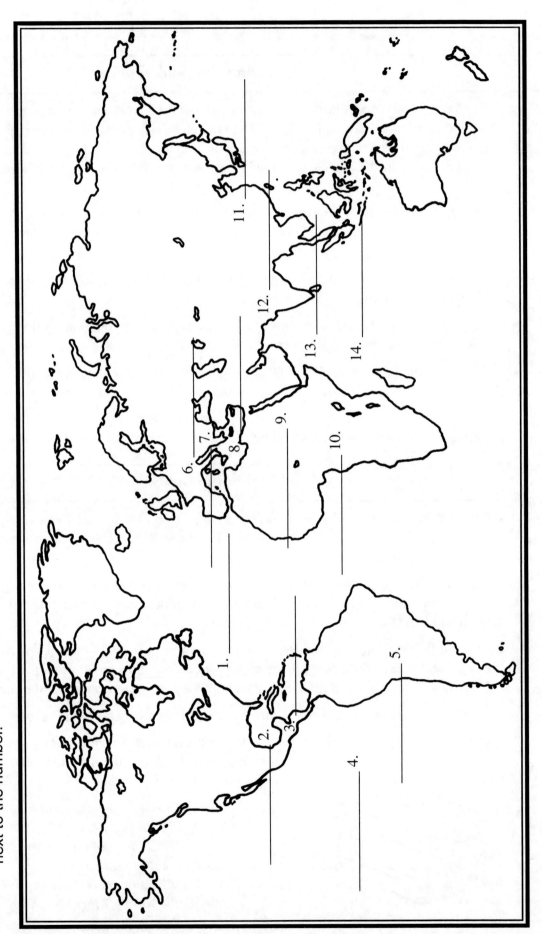

Word Knowledge

Use this activity to check students' knowledge of vocabulary from the text. First, copy the words from the box below onto the chalkboard. Next, read the first clue aloud. Direct the students to write an answer on a sheet of paper. Then reread the clue and call on a student to go to the board and circle the correct answer. Continue in this same manner until all clues have been read. Answers have been provided in parentheses as an easy reference.

relief	papyrus	excavation	obsidian
baroque	afterlife	ziggurat	forums
fresco	Linear A	Renaissance	hangtu
dendrochronology	cuneiform	trowel	thermo-luminescence
strata	occupation level	sequence dating	bucchero

1. A method of dating trees by counting growth rings *(dendrochronology)*

2. A wall painting made on wet plaster *(fresco)*

3. On an archaeological site these layers of earth may contain artifacts *(strata)*

4. This wedge-shaped writing was used by the ancient Sumerians *(cuneiform)*

5. A stratum containing material evidence of the humans who once lived there *(occupation level)*

6. The process of uncovering ancient remains *(excavation)*

7. A design chiseled into the surface of a wall *(relief)*

8. Existence after death *(afterlife)*

9. This 17th century art style features curved shapes and elaborate designs *(baroque)*

10. Sumerians built these temples crowned with a stepped tower *(ziggurat)*

11. By measuring the amount of light in clay, an artifact's age can be determined *(thermo-luminescence)*

12. Egyptians wrote on this paper made from a plant *(papyrus)*

13. Arranging objects in an order that shows how they changed over time *(sequence dating)*

14. This fine black pottery was unique to the Etruscans *(bucchero)*

15. A system of writing used by the settlers of Crete *(Linear A)*

16. Romans held meetings in these large, open market places *(forums)*

17. Excavators use this small, flat-bladed garden tool to scrape dirt *(trowel)*

18. A period of intellectual awakening in Europe during the 14th and 15th centuries *(Renaissance)*

19. This style of building is typical of early Chinese cities *(hangtu)*

20. A hard natural glass formed from rapidly cooling lava *(obsidian)*

Across the Curriculum

Extend the text with any of the following projects and activities.

Chapter 1: *Search for the Past*

Science. Experiment to find out the effects of the sun's rays on a variety of materials. Place cloth, writing paper, wood, and metal objects in direct sunlight for a period of days. Observe what happens to each object.

Art. In 1940 a group of boys in southwestern France discovered some prehistoric art in Lascaux Cave. Assign students to research the discovery (see *Kids Discover. Buried Treasure,* June/July 1994). Follow up with some cave drawings. See page 21.

Careers. Learn about other scientists and their functions at a dig site. See page 28. Have students choose jobs they would like to have at a site and explain their choices to a partner.

Science. Let students make their own models of earth's strata. Provide each small group of students with four or five different colors of modeling clay. Direct them to roll each color into a flat layer (thicknesses can vary). Pile the layers one on top of the other and gently press down. With a plastic knife cut through the center of the clay structure and pull apart to observe the different layers.

Chapter 2: *Methods of Excavation*

Critical Thinking. Test students' knowledge of four current methods of determining the age of different types of artifacts. See page 37.

Critical Thinking. Discuss excavation and why archaeologists use both horizontal and vertical methods. Speculate what might happen if archaeologists used only the horizontal method. Discuss the disadvantages of trenching.

Chapter 3: *Ancient Civilizations of the Middle East and Asia Geography.*

Geography. Direct students to draw and label a map of ancient civilizations of the Middle East and Asia. Include the Tigris and Euphrates Rivers, the Persian Gulf, Mesopotamia, the Indian and Pacific Oceans, China, Egypt, the Nile River, the Indus River Valley, and the Shang settlement.

Critical Thinking. Call attention to the chart on page 36 of *Dig This! How Archaeologists Uncover Our Past.* Note the changes as the writing gradually evolved. Have the class find examples of early 18th and 19th-century writing (e.g. the original Constitution, hornbooks, old diaries, etc.). Compare to current handwriting. Have students prepare a chart showing how today's letter formations have evolved.

Geography. Take a tour through King Tutankhamen's tomb. Learn about the treasures unearthed in 1922. See page 38. Read *Into the Mummy's Tomb* by Nicholas Reeves (Scholastic, 1992).

Chapter 4: *Ancient Civilizations of the Mediterranean*

Geography. Have groups research and draw a map of the ancient civilizations of the Mediterranean. The following should be included: Crete, Greece, the Mediterranean Sea, Africa, the Black Sea, the Roman Republic, and Mycenae.

Across the Curriculum *(cont.)*

Chapter 4: *Ancient Civilizations of the Mediterranean (cont.)*

Critical Thinking. Compare the Minoans and the Mycenaeans in a Venn diagram. Complete this activity with the whole class or let individuals complete the work sheet on page 39.

Reading. Students will enjoy learning about Greek gods and goddesses. Several versions of the *Iliad* and the *Odyssey* are available (check with your librarian), but an all-around resource is *D'Aulaire's Book of Greek Myths*.

Art. Research how reliefs were constructed. Let students experience a modern relief with the New Age Relief art project on page 40.

Critical Thinking. Read about the lost city of Pompeii and the volcano that buried the civilization there so long ago. Follow up with the six critical thinking questions on that same page (page 41).

Geography. Have groups of students research volcanoes and construct a working model or draw and label the cross-section of a volcano. An excellent resource for this project is *Janice VanCleve's Volcanoes* by Janice VanCleve (John Wiley & Sons, Inc., 1994).

Chapter 5: *Ancient Civilizations of the Americas*

Art. Observe the brightly colored jar on page 63 of *Dig This! How Archaeologists Uncover Our Past*. Note the details and colors of the jar. Let the students make their own Mayan jars. See page 40 for complete directions for this art project.

Geography. Pair or group the students. Direct them to draw a map of Mesoamerica. The following features should be labeled on the map: South America, North America, Atlantic Ocean, Pacific Ocean, Mexico, Paracas, Tiahuanaco, Guatemala, Belize, Honduras, and El Salvador. Shade in the areas in which there are sites of ancient ruins.

Chapter 6: *A Journey Through the Ages*

Geography. Archaeologists divide the history of almost every site into three distinct periods—the Stone Age, the Bronze Age, and the Iron Age. Construct a chart to show the characteristics of each age and the types of tools and weapons that might be found at a site during each age. Students can be divided into small groups for this research project.

Social Studies. Pair the students and direct them to fold a large sheet of drawing paper into thirds. Label each section with a different heading: Stone Age, Bronze Age, and Iron Age. Direct the students to chart the changes that occurred in the Holy Land through these three ages.

Art. During the Stone Age, Neolithic people made clay masks. Call attention to the example on page 72 of *Dig This! How Archaeologists Uncover Our Past*. Teach the students how to make masks with the technique on page 40.

Chapter 7: *Making Archaeology a Science*

History. Tell the students to research the Renaissance and find out ten important facts about a scholar, inventor, painter, or other famous person of the time period.

Art. A French officer found a half-buried stone tablet in Rosetta, Egypt. From this stone scholars were finally able to translate the Egyptian language. Students can make their own Rosetta Stone by following the directions on page 60 of this book.

Social Studies. Test students' knowledge of some of the early archaeologists who helped uncover secrets from the past. Use the work sheet on page 42 to assess what students know.

Across the Curriculum *(cont.)*

Chapter 7: *Making Archaeology a Science (cont.)*

Science. Sequence dating is a method employed to show how objects have changed over time. Pair the students and tell them to choose a modern object such as the television, telephone, or automobile. Instruct them to draw pictures of their chosen object from the first model to the present with some in-between pictures. Have the students share their finished projects with another group before displaying them.

Chapter 8: *Preserving the Past*

Social Studies. With the whole class discuss what they can do to preserve artifacts. Determine a class project that they can plan and carry out. Enlist your local librarian to help you find some contacts, and see Etc. on page 77 of this book for more sources.

Social Studies. Ask the students to describe the role of archaeologists in the modern world and to explain their importance to future generations.

Extensions. When you have completed reading all the chapters in *Dig This! How Archaeologists Uncover Our Past*, you may want to assign any or all of the following activities.

Math. On page 43, Ancient Math, you will find ten word problems based on information from the text of *Dig This! How Archaeologists Uncover Our Past*. Use them as a group project or assign for homework.

Creative Writing. On page 44 you will find a number of creative writing topics for students to choose from. Write two or three topics on the board at a time and give students a choice.

Social Studies. Compare ancient civilizations from different locations. For example, have students choose one site from the Middle East and Asia, one from the Mediterranean, and one from the Americas. Construct a chart and compare the civilizations. See the sample chart below.

Civilization	Sumerians	Minoans	Egyptians
Type of Writing	cuneiforms	pictographs	hieroglyphs
Main Occupations	farming	farming, trading	farming, fishing
Buildings	ziggurats	richly painted palaces	pyramids

Social Studies. Construct an Ancient Civilization Time Line. Assign each group of students a different civilization to research and have them write some facts and years on separate index cards. Let the groups work cooperatively to determine the correct chronological order of the events. Tape the cards to the chalkboard or a classroom wall.

Critical Thinking. Preview an Indiana Jones movie before showing it to the class. Afterwards, discuss some common stereotypes people may have about archaeologists, their jobs, and their looks. Let the students compare what they have learned about archaeologists with the way they were portrayed in the movie. As a follow-up, assign pairs of students to write a new adventure for Indiana Jones.

Culminating Activity. Go on a classroom dig. See pages 54 to 61.

Dating Artifacts

Help the archaeologist categorize all the words and phrases from the list below. Write each word in the correct section.

rapidly cooling lava	half-life	stores energy	absorbs water
hydration or thickness	dark rings	carbon 14	counting rings
reheat excavated	potsherds	natural glass	clay
date up to 50,000 years	ring patterns	tree trunks	living organisms

DENDROCHRONOLOGY

CARBON DATING

OBSIDIAN HYDRATION

THERMO-LUMINESCENCE

Into the Tomb

When Howard Carter entered King Tut's tomb, he was unprepared for all the sights that greeted him. Ancient treasures were piled high all around him. Among them were golden chariots, jeweled chests, vases, statues, and couches in the shapes of animals. Below is a map of all the rooms in King Tut's tomb. Read and follow the directions for a tour of the tomb and its chambers.

1.   The first room that Carter entered was the antechamber. It contained three funerary beds, two lifesize statues of a king, several chariots, a golden throne, and several ornately carved alabaster vases. Draw a chariot (or funerary bed) and a vase in the antechamber.

2.   Tutankhamen's preserved body was found in the burial chamber. The gold leaf coffin was decorated with ornate hieroglyphics and thousands of simulated precious stones. Draw a coffin in the Burial Chamber and decorate it with hieroglyphics.

3.   Within the treasury are the following features: canopic jars, a box carrying Anubis, several miniature boats, and four golden statues. Draw a boat in the treasury.

4.   Of all the rooms, the annex contained the most artifacts. There were travel beds, vanity boxes, alabaster perfume jars, games, tiny statues, and clay vessels. Fill the Annex with artifacts.

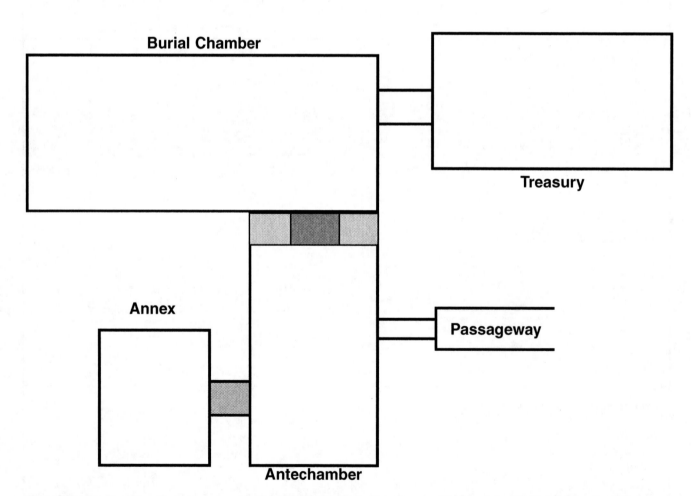

Teacher Notes: For more lessons about Egypt see Teacher Created Materials #292 Thematic Unit—*Egypt*. Also, you can see an historically accurate reproduction of King Tut's tomb at the Luxor Hotel in Las Vegas, Nevada. Artifacts are placed just as Howard Carter discovered them in 1922.

Minoans vs. Mycenaeans

Both the Minoans and the Mycenaeans were ancient civilizations of the Mediterranean region. In many respects they were alike, but in others they were vastly different. Read through the list of characteristics below. Then, write each one in the proper section of the Venn diagram.

- sailed the Mediterranean Sea

- not fortified against attack

- decorated pottery with weapons

- dead were placed in huge domed tombs

- kept a sizable navy

- settled near Athens

- settled on Crete

- Greek in origin

- flourished between 1600 B.C. to 1400 B.C.

- earliest civilization of Europe

- warriors traded goods with other settlements

- buried their dead with daggers, swords, and shields

- produced wine and olive oil

- *Iliad* and *Odyssey* were set in this period

- flourished between 2000 B.C. and 1400 B.C.

- had richly painted and decorated houses

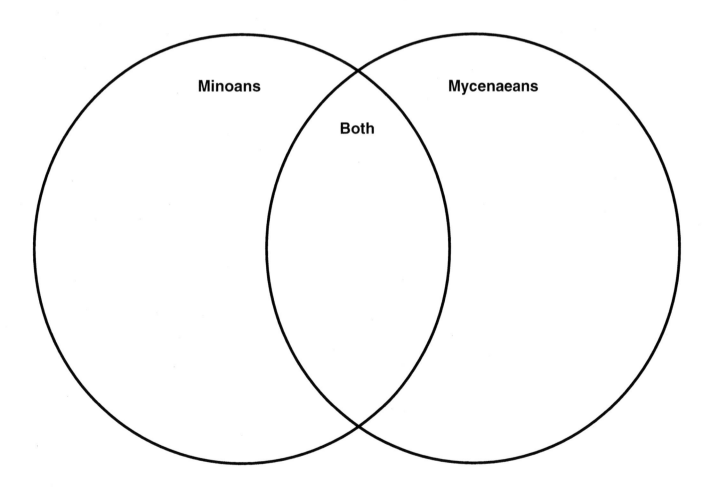

Ancient Art Projects

Coordinate these art projects with the reading of the chapters. Make a relief after reading Chapter 4, create Mayan jars for Chapter 5, and construct masks after reading Chapter 6.

New Age Relief. A relief is a type of sculpture in which forms and figures are chiseled from the surface of a wall. Student pairs or groups can make a modern version of a relief with this project.

Materials: various sizes of cardboard boxes, small toys and objects, white glue or glue gun, cardboard (cut one side from a large box), spray paint (any color)

Directions:

1. Glue the objects to the cardboard and allow to dry.
2. Take the relief outdoors and spray paint.
3. Allow plenty of time to dry before displaying in the classroom.

Mayan Jars. Observe the Mayan jar on page 63 of *Dig This! How Archaeologists Uncover Our Past.* Note the designs and colors employed. Let the students make their own Mayan jars.

Materials: clean glass jars or plastic bottles, colored art tissue or wrapping paper, scissors, white glue mixed with some water, brushes, fine-line black marking pen

Directions:

1. Cover the jar or bottle with glue and press one layer of tissue paper onto the bottle.
2. Brush some glue over the surface.
3. Cut out designs from the tissue and press onto the background. Brush with glue.
4. Continue in the same manner until the surface of the jar or bottle is completely covered.
5. After drying, draw some features with the fine-line marking pen.

Masks. During the Stone Age the art of making pottery was developed. People of this era also began to mold clay into masks. Students can create clay masks with this project.

Materials: clay or homemade dough (In a bowl combine 1 ½ cups (375 mL) each of flour and cornmeal and 1 cup (250 mL) each of salt and water. Mix thoroughly; add more water if necessary.), black marking pens, cleaned plastic bleach bottles, scissors, tempera paints
Directions:

1. With the pen draw the outline of a mask on the surface of the bottle.
2. Use the scissors to cut out the mask from the plastic bottle.
3. Cover the plastic with a thin layer of clay.
4. Make holes for eyes, nose, and mouth.
5. Allow to dry.
6. Carefully remove the plastic and add painted features painted with tempera.

Pompeii

Use this story to develop critical thinking skills. Assign students to read the paragraphs. On a separate sheet of paper, write answers to the questions that follow. Check and discuss the answers with the whole group.

In A.D. 79 Pompeii was a small but busy Roman city located on the Bay of Naples. Overlooking the city was a mountain called Mt. Vesuvius. This mountain was actually a volcano, but Pompeii's 20 to 30 thousand inhabitants were unaware of the danger lurking beneath the green vegetation of its slopes. Primarily a commercial and agricultural town, Pompeii was prosperous due in large part to its location. Its two ports allowed the people to trade with other Roman towns and with the distant empires of Egypt and Spain. The area's fertile soil and mild climate contributed to its success as an agricultural center. Grain, grapes, wine, olives, sheep, and flowers were among the variety of crops raised.

Suddenly, the peaceful scene changed as Mt. Vesuvius violently erupted. A few years earlier in A.D. 62, an earthquake had rocked southern Italy but the energetic Pompeiians had quickly rebuilt their city. There had been no volcanic activity then, but on August 24, A.D. 79, a deafening sound filled the air. It was about 1 p.m. and many Pompeiians were eating lunch. As the top of Mt. Vesuvius blasted off, volcanic rock ash and red-hot stones shot thousands of feet into the air. Fire, smoke, and molten lava poured out of the volcano's mouth. So much dust was produced that the sun was blotted out. The sea filled up with volcanic deposits and swelled up in giant waves. Fiery surges roared down the volcano five more times in the 11 hours after the first explosion. The final ones spread through the walls of Pompeii, knocking people over. Other residents were asphyxiated by the poisonous gases emitted by the volcanic matter. When it was all over, the city lay buried and almost forgotten until the mid 1700s.

Knowledge: When did Pompeii flourish? Where was it located? What was Mt. Vesuvius?

Comprehension: In your own words, explain what happened when Mt. Vesuvius erupted. Name two factors that contributed to the prosperity of the city.

Application: What would happen if Mt. Vesuvius were to explode today? Would the outcome be any different? Defend your answer.

Analysis: Identify the main ideas of the story. Write three different titles which would convey the main idea of this article.

Synthesis: Pretend you were an eyewitness to the eruption. Write about the sights, sounds, smells, and other sensations of the event.

Evaluation: Compare the eruption of Mt. Vesuvius with modern volcanic activity such as Mt. St. Helens in Washington (May 18, 1980), Kilauea in Hawaii (erupting since 1983), or Krakatau in Indonesia (1883).

Early Archaeologists

Test your knowledge of early archaeologists. Read the clues on the first line and circle the correct answer on the line next line.

1. French emperor/Rosetta stone/1799

    Jean-Francis Champollion   Napoleon Bonaparte   Charles Darwin

2. German/millionaire at 41/*Iliad* and *Odyssey*

    Arthur Evans   Pliny   Heinrich Schliemann

3. potsherds/strata-dating system/sequence dating

    Augustus Pitt-Rivers   Flinders Petrie   Bernard de Montfaucon

4. theory of evolution/lower primates/British

    Charles Darwin   Georg Grotefund   Flinders Petrie

5. artifact guide/1764/German

    Johann Winckelmann   Arthur Evans   Howard Carter

6. cuneiform writing/German/Mesopotamia

    Heinrich Schliemann   Augustus Pitt-Rivers   Georg Grotefund

7. Tutankhamen tomb/British/archaeologist

    Otto I   Howard Carter   Napoleon Bonaparte

8. Minoan culture/Knossos/financed own research

    Bernard de Montfaucon   Arthur Evans   Homer

9. French scholar/Rosetta stone/deciphered hieroglyphic script

    Napoleon Bonaparte   Jean-Francois Champollion   Archbishop Usser

10. systematic/meticulous recording/rapid publication of findings

    Titus   Johann Winckelmann   Augustus Pitt-Rivers

11. plastered the hollows/Italian/Pompeii

    Giuseppe Fiorelli   Archbishop Usser   Pliny

12. King of Greece/1832/excavated Greek temples

    Jean-Frances Champollion   Titus   Otto I

From the names above choose the person that you think has contributed most to the science of archaeology. Write the name on the line provided. In the space that follows defend your choice.

_____

Archaeologist

Ancient Math

The following math problems are based on facts and figures from the text of *Dig This! How Archaeologists Uncover Our Past.* Give a copy of this page to each group of students to complete together. Direct them to show their work on separate paper. When all the groups have completed this page, orally check the answers and processes used to determine them.

1. The Sumerians occupied southwest Mesopotamia from about 4000 B.C. to 2300 B.C. How many years did they occupy the area?

2. The Parthenon is 237 feet long and 110 feet wide. What is the area of the Parthenon? Hint: Area = length x width.

3. Teotihuacan was a massive urban hub that stretched over 5 square miles and housed more than 20,000 people. On the average, how many people lived in each square mile?

4. Arthur Evans began excavating the palace of the Minoan kings in 1906 and continued his work for 35 years. In what year did he complete his work?

5. The Parthenon is 237 feet long, 110 feet wide, and 60 feet high. What is the volume of this structure? Hint: Volume = length x width x height.

6. Gudea ruled the Sumerian city-state of Lagah from 2144 to 2124 B.C. How many years was Gudea ruler of Lagah?

7. Mt. Vesuvius erupted in 79 A.D., burying Pompeii which was not rediscovered until 1728. How many years passed before it was found?

8. The ancient city of Tikal covers more than 9 square miles in the rain forests of Guatemala. What is the length of one side of the city?

9. The Pyramid of the Sun stands approximately 200 feet high while the Parthenon is 60 feet high. What is the difference in height between the two?

10. The Parthenon is 110 feet wide and 237 feet long. What is the perimeter of the Parthenon? Hint: Perimeter = 2 x length + 2 x width.

Creative Writing Topics

Combine creative writing and critical thinking with the following writing assignments. Give students a choice of topics from the list below or assign a specific topic for everyone.

1. You have just discovered a new artifact from the ancient Shang empire. Draw a picture of the artifact and tell what you think it was used for.

2. After reading Pliny's eyewitness account of the Mt. Vesuvius eruption, write a newspaper headline and accompanying article about the event.

3. Write a list of tools that are necessary on a dig. Explain how each one is used in an actual excavation.

4. Find a picture of an actual mural that depicts Egyptian life and describe everything that is happening in the picture.

5. You are Howard Carter and have just found the tomb of Tutankhamen. Write 15 things you might have said as you entered and then searched through the chambers.

6. Write a creative story that tells how Giuseppi Fiorelli developed his technique to recreate the hollow spaces found in the buried rubble at Pompeii.

7. Sumerians drew pictographs or pictures to stand for words and ideas. Invent 20 modern pictographs and use them to write a story about modern life.

8. Use all of the following words in a creative story about ancient civilizations: artifacts, strata, carbon dating, cuneiforms, papyrus, legends, and Iron Age.

9. It is believed that Shang kings inscribed bones and turtle shells with questions to their ancestors. On a large sheet of drawing paper draw the outline of a bone. Within the shape write questions to your ancestors.

10. Archaeologists employ many methods of determining the age of artifacts. You have just invented a new dating method. Write a name for this method and explain how it works.

11. Ancient Romans often met at public baths. Write a conversation two men might have had as they discussed the planned drainage system or the newly installed aqueduct.

12. Would you rather have been a Minoan or a Mycenaean? Defend your choice in a two or three paragraph answer.

13. Compare the architecture of an Egyptian ziggurat with that of the Acropolis. Discuss how the buildings were constructed and the purposes of each.

14. Choose from one of the following ancient civilizations and write about a day in the life of a typical citizen: Shang, Minoan, Roman, Mayan, Olmec, Sumerian, Egyptian, or the Indus River Valley.

15. It is the year 3000 and archaeologists have just discovered a town that appears to have been buried since 1995. Write a story about the artifacts that are uncovered and explain what they tell about the lifestyle then.

Mesopotamia Unit

The following section contains a unit of study on ancient Mesopotamia. A number of suggested ways to use the pages appear below. Adapt, add, and delete any of the following ideas to suit your classroom goals and student needs.

*Introducing the Topic.

Read aloud selections from either of the following books: *In the Land of Ur* by Hans Baumann (Pantheon Books, 1969); *The Faraway Lurs* by Harry Behn (Gregg Press, 1981). Stop reading at an interesting juncture so that students will be eager to know more. (Note: Although both of these books are out of print, they may be available at the public or even your school library.)

*Make Individual Learning Packets.

1. Reproduce enough copies of pages 46 to 53 to make one booklet for each student. If you prefer, make one booklet per pair or group of students to complete together.
2. Have each student make a cover for his/her book by folding a 12-inch by 18-inch (30cm x 45cm) sheet of construction paper in half.
3. Have students list a table of contents on a sheet of notebook paper.
4. Compile all the pages in numerical order and place them between the cover; staple three or four times along the left edge.
5. Students may work on their own to complete the learning packet during free time or a specially designated time period.
6. Provide an answer key for self-checking by copying the answers for those pages from the Answer Key on page 79. Appoint a different student each day to be an "answer checker."

*Archaeology Center Packets.

Make two or three packets from pages 46 to 53 for your archaeology center.

1. After copying, glue each page to index or heavy card stock; laminate and trim.
2. Compile the pages into separate booklets. Punch holes along one side with a three-hole punch.
3. Attach hole reinforcers to both sides of all holes before adding the pages to a three-ring binder.
4. Keep the packets at your classroom archaeology center for students to work on during designated times.

*Incorporate Into Lesson Plans.

If your curriculum and/or social studies text already contains information about Mesopotamia, use the pages in this section as support material as needed.

 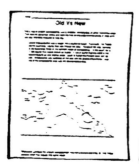 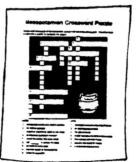 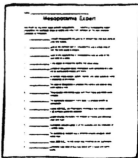

Name_____

Mesopotamia Expert

How much do you know about ancient Mesopotamia? To become a Mesopotamia expert, unscramble the boldfaced group of letters and write them correctly on the lines provided. Capitalize as necessary.

1. _____Ancient Mesopotamia included all of present-day Iraq plus parts of Syria and **yurket.**

2. _____Land in the northern part of Mesopotamia was a broad area of high, flat land called a **letapua.**

3. _____Much of the southern half of Mesopotamia was an area of flat, open land or a **ilpna.**

4. _____In the region of **mesur** the world's first cities arose.

5. _____Centers of population called **iytc-taesst** were composed of a city and its surrounding villages and farms.

6. _____An **sartina** made jewelry, pottery, fabrics, and other goods by hand to exchange at the market.

7. _____The story of **Gilgamesh** is probably the world's first **pice** or long poem about a hero.

8. _____Those people who moved about with their flocks and herds were **somand.**

9. _____The Sumerians believed in many gods—a practice known as **eipylsotmh.**

10. _____Around 900 B.C., the Phoenicians invented a new writing system of 22 symbols called the **pateblah.**

11. _____Sargon created the world's first **mepier** of nations and city-state under one ruler.

12. _____Hammurabi brought justice to all his subjects with the institution of a central **deco.**

13. _____The **gurgzita** at Babylon was a pyramid-shaped structure seven stories high.

14. _____About 3500 B.C., the first **leweh** was invented by the Sumerians.

15. _____Sumerians kept track of business deals with a **lulab** and some tokens.

Mesopotamia

Name_____

Old Vs New

Find a map of ancient Mesopotamia. Use a textbook, encyclopedia, or other reference book. Then read the paragraph below and label the map on this page with the words in bold print. Use your reference resource to help you.

Ancient **Mesopotamia** was a region, not a country or nation. Two rivers, the **Tigris** and the Euphrates, wound their way through the area. The city of **Hit** was founded on the **Euphrates River** in the northern region of Mesopotamia. To the south lay a 10,000 square mile region known as **Sumer.** It was in Sumer that the world's first cities—including **Ur** and **Kish**— arose. South of Sumer the **Persian Gulf** can be seen. Mesopotamia was bordered on the east with the **Zagros Mountains.** Due west of the Mesopotamia area was the **Mediterranean Sea.**

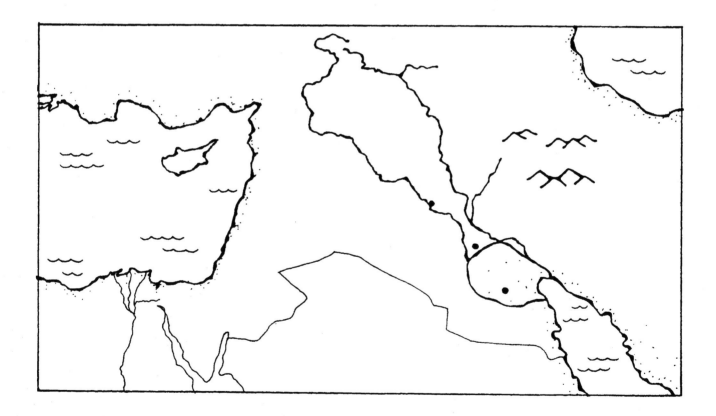

*Challenge: Compare the ancient Mesopotamian map with a present-day map to find those countries which now occupy that same region.

Name_____

Mesopotamian Crossword Puzzle

Review your knowledge of Mesopotamian culture with this crossword puzzle. You may want to work with a partner to complete the puzzle.

Across

2. professional writers and record keepers
5. the mother goddess
7. system of channeling water to the fields
9. an important Sumerian invention
11. where the world's first cities arose
12. high _____; he served the gods
13. the belief in many gods
14. one river border of Mesopotamia
15. center of population

Down

1. legendary hero who was king of Uruk
3. an organized set of laws
4. the god of the air
6. products of human imagination
8. they worked with their herds
10. pictures that stand for words
14. a long poem about a hero

Name_____

Civilization Features

A civilization is a complex society that exhibits five features. To find out these features, solve each problem in the Problem Box. Find the answers below the spaces and write the corresponding letter on the line.

Some letters and words have been provided for you.

Problem Box

g=850 ÷ 25	d=860 ÷ 43	v=594 ÷ 18
s = 735 ÷ 21	p=572 ÷ 26	l=779 ÷ 41
t= 432 ÷ 16	c=644 ÷ 23	b=702 ÷ 18
n=518 ÷ 14	h=540 ÷ 30	z=713 ÷ 31
f=4000 ÷ 10	r=651 ÷ 31	m=756 ÷ 21

---

1. ____ ____ a ____ ____ e ____ o o ____ ____ u ____ ____ ____ y
   35   27   39 19   40   20   35   22   22   19

2. ____ ____ e ____ i a ____ i ____ a ____ i o ____   of   ____ a ____ o ____
   35   22   28   19   23   27   37   19   39   21

3. system of ____ o ____ e ____ ____ ____ e ____ ____
             34   33 21   37 36 37 27

4. ____ o ____ i a ____ ____ e ____ e ____ ____
   35   28   19   19   33   19   35

5. ____ i ____ ____ ____ y developed ____ u ____ ____ u ____ e that includes
   18   34   18   19   28   19   27   21

  a ____ ____ , ____ e ____ i ____ i o ____ , ____ u ____ i ____ , and law.
    21   27   21   19   34   37   36   35   28

Mesopotamia

Hammurabi's New Code

When Hammurabi came to power in Babylonia in 1792 B.C., he proved to be a capable and powerful leader, a wise king, and a great military commander.

Among all those accomplishments, he is mainly remembered for one achievement—the Code of Hammurabi. These laws covered religion, irrigation, trade, property, slavery, family matters, crime, and more. For example, one law said that if a freeman destroyed the eye of another freeman, his eye should be destroyed. Another law proclaimed that if a freeman hired an ox and destroyed its eye, he would have to give one-half of the value of the ox in silver to the owner.

Find a list of some other laws set forth by Hammurabi. Look in an encyclopedia or a history text. On the lines below copy any five of those laws. Next to each one, rewrite it to fit today's society.

1. _____

_____

_____

2. _____

_____

_____

3. _____

_____

_____

4. _____

_____

_____

5. _____

_____

_____

Cracking the Code

This ancient clay tablet contains an inscription that has not yet been deciphered. Decode the message by using the cuneiform clues at the bottom of this page. Note: Cuneiform was a system of writing developed before modern alphabets. They were characters that stood for both words or syllables. These symbols are only representational of true cuneiform writing.

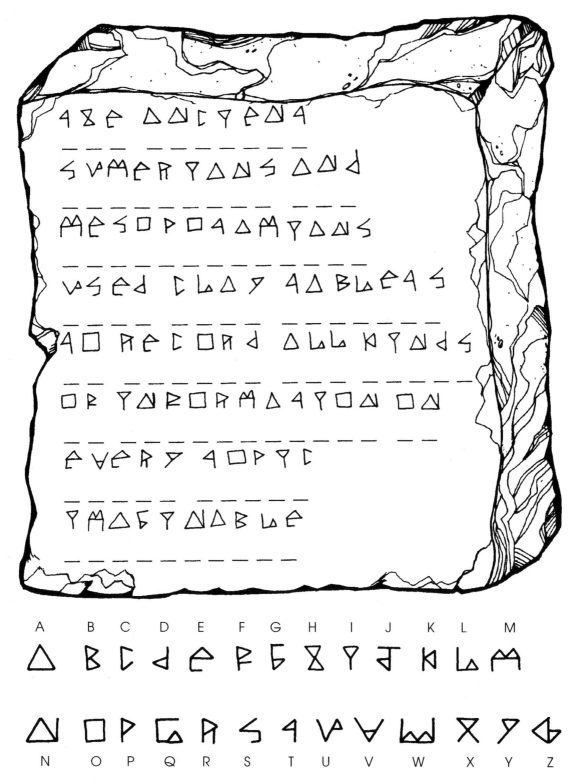

Cause and Effect

Cause and effect are terms that explain relationships between two events. Cause tells the reason something happened, while effect shows the resulting thing that happens.

Look at the following sentence: The woman opened her umbrella because it began to rain. In this sentence the cause is the rain; the effect is that the woman opened up her umbrella.

Examine each sentence below. Write the causes and the effects on the lines provided.

1. Sumer gave rise to the world's first civilization because irrigation allowed farmers to produce a surplus of food.

   cause: _____

   effect: _____

2. Some people were able to work at an occupation other than farming since there was a surplus of food.

   cause: _____

   effect: _____

3. The Sumerians invented the sailboat because they needed to transport goods to trade with other peoples.

   cause: _____

   effect: _____

4. The Sumerians felt helpless against the forces of nature so they tried their best to please the gods.

   cause: _____

   effect: _____

5. Because of very little rain and heavy spring floods, the Sumerians created an irrigation system.

   cause: _____

   effect: _____

6. Writing was invented by the Sumerian traders because they needed an accurate method of recording what they bought and sold.

   cause: _____

   effect: _____

Challenge: On the lines below list some things that might have caused the fall of the empire.

_____

_____

_____

Ancient Mesopotamia and Science

Not only was Mesopotamia the oldest civilization, it was also the birthplace of early science and technology. Read about some of the Sumerian scientific accomplishments below; extension activities follow each one.

The Body. Sumerian physicians probably gathered information about the human body from their studies of victims of accidents and wars. The heart was important, they knew, and it was considered to be the center of thought and knowledge. Another organ, the liver, was even more highly regarded. They considered it to be the center of emotions and life itself. So intrigued were the Sumerians by the liver that they gave special names to each of its five lobes and made clay models of it for a reference tool.

Extension: Draw and label a human heart and a liver; describe the functions of each.

Disease. The basis of many medical treatments in ancient Mesopotamia was trial and error or folk remedies. In addition, these treatments relied on superstition and magic. For example, the Babylonians believed that fevers were caused by a demon who entered and then devoured the body. Even if a patient was treated with ointment or herbs, a real cure could only be obtained by pacifying the appropriate god.

Extension: Write two or three folk remedies for curing the common cold, hiccups, or a fever.

Surgery. Although surgery was not widely practiced at this time, some evidence exists that supports a procedure called *trephination*. In cases where the brain would swell inside the skull, surgeons were able to relieve pressure by cutting out a small section of the skull. This piece was replaced once the swelling subsided.

Extension: Find out if trephination is used by modern surgeons. What are the latest techniques used by brain surgeons?

Drugs. Physicians of this era relied on plant, animal, and mineral matter for ingredients in the drugs they developed. Salt, a common ingredient, was also used as an antiseptic to clean wounds. Other sources of drugs included the seeds, roots, branches, and bark of pear, fig, and date trees. Some prescriptions called for milk, snakeskin, and turtle shell.

Extension: Find out what plants are used in the production of these medicines: quinine, aspirin, codeine, and taxol. Name some other plants used for medicinal purposes.

On Your Own: Read *Science in Ancient Mesopotamia* by Carol Moss (Franklin Watts, 1988).

Going on a Dig

No doubt about it—a dig simulation requires a lot of planning and preparation. It is a more-than-worthwhile educational activity, and students will likely remember it for a long time to come. Often, though, the necessary resources, time, and facilities needed for a successful dig are unavailable to the teacher or the school. With those limitations in mind, this dig simulation has been devised for you.

This compact eight-page guide (pages 53 to 61) will help you cut down on the planning time; and, once you have all your learning materials in order, it will be easy to follow the step-by-step directions. Sample work sheets are also provided for use at your discretion. Read through all the directions below and on page 55 before embarking on this adventure. Choose those activities which are most appropriate for your classroom.

I. PREVIEW

1. **Set the Mood.** Give students an idea of what is coming by displaying books such as *Digging the Past* by Bruce Porell (Addison-Wesley, 1979), *Going on a Dig* by Velma Ford Morrison (Dodd, Mead & Company, 1981), or *Digging to the Past* by W.John Hackwell (Charles Scribner's Sons, 1986). For more titles, see the bibliography on page 80. Read portions of these books aloud to students to garner interest.

   Another way to set the mood is to plan a field trip to an archaeological museum or, if possible, to an actual dig site. Back in the classroom discuss what was observed, the methods used to find artifacts, etc.

2. **Group the students.** Divide students into two teams balanced as evenly as possible by ability and sex. Select a strong, reliable leader for each team.

3. **Maintain private areas for the groups to construct their artifacts if possible.** An aide or parent volunteer, if available, can take one group at a time to a resource room or other school space. If the students must remain in the classroom, create a room-divider with a refrigerator box or hang a sheet from the ceiling. Student groups can take turns working in this designated area.

4. **Find a desirable spot to conduct the dig.** Two alternatives: Make chalk grids on a large blacktop area of the playground or push back the desks and tape two separate grids—one for each team—to the classroom floor. Directions are on page 56.

5. **Gather all the necessary materials.** On page 60 you will find lists of items needed to complete the art-related projects. Materials for the dig can be found at the top of page 56.

6. **Make copies** of the necessary forms for assignments. (See pages 58 and 59.)

II. OVERVIEW

Now that all necessary materials are organized and ready to go, discuss with the students what is going to happen throughout this dig simulation. Establish the following points:

1. Both teams will be creating their own culture from the past, present, or future. Give each team a copy of the Culture Report work sheet on page 58. Discuss it with the students; make sure they know what is expected of them.

2. In addition to creating a culture, students will be making some appropriate artifacts for the culture. Ideas are outlined on page 60.

Going on a Dig *(cont.)*

OVERVIEW *(cont.)*

3. Emphasize that this is a cooperative group effort and that everyone will have an important role to play. (See Roles, below.)

4. One group will be competing with the other to find information about the opposite team's culture. Therefore, emphasize that students are not to discuss their team project with members of the opposing team.

III. ROLES

Some students will share a role, while others may be more suited to a separate responsibility. All students will participate in group discussions. Suggested jobs and duties are outlined below.

1. One student in each team should be chosen by the teacher to be the **team leader.** The team leader moderates group discussions.

2. The whole team can select a **recorder or secretary** to record notes during group discussions and during the dig itself.

3. **Artisans** can be appointed to make the artifacts on page 60.

4. **Mural artists** will also be needed to complete a picture of the mythical culture.

5. Three or four **scribes** may devise an alphabet for their culture.

6. Two or more **measurers** will be needed to construct the squares of the site.

7. **One or two students with cameras** (instant, camcorders, or otherwise) will photograph the unearthed artifacts.

8. In addition to the photographers, one or two **artists** can be employed to draw sketches of the artifacts from the dig.

9. Name other roles as the need arises.

IV Sample Lesson Plans

I. Give students an overview of the project. Tell them they will be divided into two competing groups or teams. Each team is going to create a new culture. The groups will try to learn all they can about the other group's culture from artifacts found in a dig.

II. Divide the students into two groups and explain the various jobs and duties that students will have within their team. (See above.)

III. Distribute the Culture Report and blank work sheet (pages 57 and 58). Review it with students; discuss any questions or problems.

IV. Have the students work on the various aspects of the project—art, written report, alphabet, etc.

V. Prepare the dig site. See page 56 for ideas.

VI. Conduct the dig. Tag and record the artifacts. See page 59 for forms. Draw pictures, and take photographs.

VII. Write a report on the newly-unearthed culture. Use a Culture Report, page 58.

Preparing the Dig

The Dig Site

Choose the appropriate directions for preparing the dig site. Students may prepare their own pits; and, in the process, have some measuring experiences. An added bonus is working as a cooperative group.

A. Concrete or Blacktop. For each team you will need a measuring stick or tape measure and chalk. For each pit measure a ten-foot (3m) by twelve-foot (3.65m) area; draw the perimeter lines. Draw 120 one-foot (.30m) squares within those lines. Establish a grid system and mark the appropriate squares. (See the diagram at right.)

	A	B	C	D
1				
2				
3				

B. Indoors. Push back the desks to create plenty of space for two pits. Each team will need a measuring stick or tape measure and masking tape. Determine how large the squares will be. (Size will vary according to the room's dimensions.) Make the perimeter lines and interior lines using the masking tape.

Conducting the Dig

1. Have each team gather its artifacts in a box. Keep the opposite team out of the area while the other team is setting up its site. When artifacts have been placed on the grid, direct the group to draw a map or blueprint of the site on graph paper. Cover the complete site with a sheet or large tablecloth. Allow the other team to prepare in the same manner. (For a touch of authenticity, pour a light layer of flour over the artifacts and replace the covering before students begin the dig.)

2. When both dig sites have been prepared, the teams may remove the cover from the opposite team's site. Have the photographer (if there is one) immediately take pictures of the area. Remind the students to fill out an artifact form for each object found before removing it from the grid. Attach an identifying tag on each find before putting it in a large box (the same one that was used to carry items to the site). Sample Artifact Forms and ID Tags can be found on page 59.

3. Back at the "lab" (classroom), examination of the artifacts begins. The language experts try to crack the code, the artists draw pictures of the artifacts, the recorder makes a list of the artifacts, and the remaining students interpret the data (artifacts, Rosetta stone, mural, etc.). Direct them to discuss all the clues they have found to complete a culture report. Blank forms are on page 58.

4. Have one team present its findings to the other team. Tell them to compare their finished culture report with the actual one made by the opposing team. Now have the two teams exchange roles.

5. Direct each team to compile its artifact forms and the resulting culture report into a book. Display the books along with their corresponding artifacts.

Culture Report

Your group is going to create a new, unheard, of culture. All the information that you will be required to supply is listed below. Use this page as a guide to help you invent information about the culture. Write your report in a notebook or on separate sheets of paper with at least one page for each topic. (Topics are in bold print.) Write the topic at the top of each page; include pictures and diagrams.

Name your culture. It can be a word spelled backwards, a slang term with a prefix or suffix added, or a newly-invented word.

1. **Time.** Choose a time for your culture; it could be past, present, or future. Describe the geographic features of the area (desert, mountain, rivers, etc.) Write a physical description of the people; be sure to include drawings or pictures of them.

2. **Values/Rules.** Make a list of their values and the rules by which they conducted their lives. Tell what was most important to these people (family life, money, intelligence, etc.).

3. **Technology.** Tell about the advances they made in technology; draw pictures of any new devices. Also describe and draw pictures of their methods of transportation.

4. **Foods/Fashion/Shelter.** Write a typical daily menu; explain how most foods were produced (test tubes; recycled foods; etc.). Draw pictures of the latest fashion craze for both men and women. Tell about the living conditions and describe a typical home.

5. **Government.** Choose a form of government for the culture (monarchy, dictatorship, etc.) and tell how officials are chosen. Explain how laws were enforced; write some important laws established by the culture.

6. **Marriage/Family.** Explain how marriage partners were chosen. Describe the typical family. Tell about the child-rearing practices of the time. (Perhaps children were sent to a co-op until they were school-age.)

7. **Religious Beliefs.** Describe any religious beliefs and practices these people held. Write step-by-step directions explaining how they buried their dead.

8. **Alphabet/Language.** Create an alphabet and a language for the culture. Also devise a number system.

9. **Art/Music/Dance.** Tell what kind of art was popular then (little use of color; abstracts; etc.). Describe the music that was popular; tell about the latest dance craze; list some books that were on the best-seller list.

10. **Games/Leisure**. Make up a game that the children liked to play. Describe the national sport. Tell how people used their leisure time.

Culture Report

Group Members: _____

_____

_____

Name of Culture: _____

1. Time: _____

    _____

2. Values/Rules: _____

    _____

3. Technology: _____

    _____

4. Foods/Fashion/Shelter: _____

    _____

5. Government: _____

    _____

6. Marriage/Family: _____

    _____

7. Religious Beliefs: _____

    _____

8. Alphabet/Language: _____

    _____

9. Art/Music/Dance: _____

    _____

10. Games/Leisure: _____

    _____

Artifact Forms/ID Tags

Name: _____

Date: _____

Description of Artifact: _____

_____

Any Markings on Artifact: _____

Translation of Markings: _____

Possible Uses of Artifact: _____

What It Represents: _____

Draw a side view and a front view of the artifact on the back.

ID Tag: _____

Describe the artifact: _____

Location found: _____

Recorder: _____

ID Tag: _____

Describe the artifact: _____

Location found: _____

Recorder: _____

Making Artifacts

Both teams will need to create three different types of artifacts—a mural, a "Rosetta Stone," and everyday objects. Some suggested methods are outlined below.

Mural. A group mural should contain examples of each of the elements listed in the culture report (page 57). Simple pictures of people at work, play, and in their home may be included. Messages or labels should be written in the language and numerals that have been developed by the group for their culture.

Materials: butcher paper, an opened grocery sack, or a piece of cloth; choice of paints, colored marking pens, chalk, and other materials depends on the time period the students are trying to recreate.

Directions:

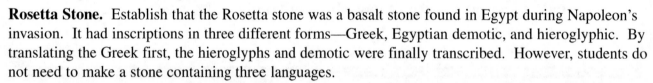

* Draw the designs, figures, and messages to represent the culture. Use any of the drawing materials listed.
* When the mural is complete, it can be torn into a number of pieces (but not too many!) to be placed on the dig site.

Rosetta Stone. Establish that the Rosetta stone was a basalt stone found in Egypt during Napoleon's invasion. It had inscriptions in three different forms—Greek, Egyptian demotic, and hieroglyphic. By translating the Greek first, the hieroglyphs and demotic were finally transcribed. However, students do not need to make a stone containing three languages.

Materials: clay or a large sheet of tagboard; rolling pin (for the clay); paper clip, wood cuticle stick, wood ice cream stick, or unsharpened pencil; colored pencils, crayons, or markers; scissors.

Directions:

* Roll the clay to a one-fourth inch (.6cm) thickness; shape as desired. If using tagboard, cut to the desired shape.
* Inscribe the clay with an opened paper clip, a wood cuticle stick, a wood ice cream stick, or an unsharpened pencil.
* Write a message in both the language of the culture and in English. Use colored pencils, crayons, or markers to write on the tagboard.
* When the clay is dry, break it up into three or four pieces to be placed on the dig site; cut the tagboard into a few sections.

Everyday Objects.

Materials: plaster of Paris or clay; paper clips, pencils, or other carving objects; hammer; paper sack.

Directions:

* Tell the groups to determine some everyday objects that they want represented at the dig.
* Make scale samples of them from plaster of Paris or clay.
* Engrave designs or messages with paper clips, etc.
* After the artifacts have dried, place them one at a time in a paper sack. With a hammer, break them apart into two to four pieces that can easily be fitted together again.

Going on a Dig Extensions

After all the hard work you and your class have put into conducting a dig, you may want to reward everyone with one of these surprise projects. They are fun to do and will be very rewarding!

Treasure Candles. Pyramid candles with small treasures hidden inside can be purchased from candle shops or gift stores. They are great fun—as the candle burns, the buried tokens are revealed. The only drawback to these is the price—even one for the whole class may be beyond your budget. So here are the directions for creating your own hidden treasure candles.

Materials: paraffin wax; double boiler; clean, empty pint-sized cardboard containers; petroleum jelly; aluminum foil; small birthday candles; small trinkets (pieces of old jewelry, metal items such as paper clips, nuts and bolts, or nails, game tokens, or miniature dollhouse artifacts, etc.);

Directions:

* Wrap each trinket separately in aluminum foil; set aside.
* Spread a layer of petroleum jelly inside the cardboard containers.
* Melt the wax in the top section of a double boiler. Be very cautious as the wax will "pop" if it becomes too hot.
* Pour a layer of wax in the bottom of the cardboard container.
* Carefully drop in four or five trinkets.
* Fill the container three-fourths full with the melted wax.
* When the wax starts to thicken, place a candle in the center of the wax.
* After the wax has hardened, tear away the cardboard container, light the candle, and collect the treasures.

Archaeology Boxes

Students will be able to enjoy their own private dig with this idea.

Materials:

* empty shoe boxes or other small boxes; foam packing pieces or popcorn or cotton batting; small trinkets (see trinket list from above); aluminum foil or plastic wrap

Directions:

* Separately wrap each trinket in aluminum foil or plastic wrap.
* Cover the bottom of the box with the packing pieces.
* Sprinkle some trinkets over this layer.
* Cover with more packing pieces. (More layers can be added in the same manner, if desired.)
* Cover the boxes with their lids. Distribute them to the students and let them dig out their prizes.
* If you are planning to invite parents to view your class dig and archaeology unit, have the students prepare the boxes. Guests may keep the treasures that they find.

Vocabulary List

This handy reference can be used in a number of ways: As a word bank for creative writing, rhymes, and poems; as a list of geography and social studies terms to know; and as a model for spelling and vocabulary development. Add to this list throughout the unit of studies.

Famous Archaeologists

Thomas Jefferson
Sir Leonard Wooley
Howard Carter
Hiram Bingham
Dame Kathleen Kenyon
Sir W.M. Flinders Petrie
Augustus Lane-Fox Pitt Rivers
Heinrich Schliemann
John Aubrey
Mary Leakey
Louis Leakey
Eugene Dubois
Henri Breuil
Raymond Dart

Early Humans

Hittites
Homo erectus
Homo habilis
Cro-Magnon
Ice Age hunters
Bronze Age
hominids
Stone Age
Sumerians
Babylonians
Java humans
Neanderthal
Modern humans
Homo Sapiens
hunter-gatherers
Piltdown humans
Iron Age
"Lucy"
Tollund humans
Paleoliothic humans
australopithecines
Peking humans

Places and Structures

Hanging Gardens of Babylonia
Altamira, Spain Mesopotamia
moai on Easter Island
Pompeii and Mt. Vesuvius
Lescaux Cave, France
Pyramids of Egypt
Fertile Crescent
Catal Huyuk
Olduvai Gorge
Koster Site
Ur
Kish
Uruk
Nipur
aqueducts
Ziggurat
Stonehenge
Ishtar Gate
megaliths
Babylonia

Artifacts and Tools

pottery and pot shards
flint tools and weapons
shell and bone bracelets
fire making
burial mounds
cave paintings
cowrie shells (as money)
clay tablets
kitchen midden
fire
coins
arrowheads
hand-axe
awls
papyrus
carvings
stylus
bola
fossils
wheel
bulla
sherd
pictographs, cuneiform, and hieroglyphics

Other Terms

Tigris and Euphrates Rivers
Code of Hammurabi
Pythagorean Theorem
sexagesimal system
potassium-argon dating
thermoluminescence
Carolus Linnaeus
prehistoric
strata
shekel
straigraphy
photography
radiocarbon dating
dendrochronology
prehistory
Shamshi-Adad
Nebuchadnezzar
Chaldeans
Hammurabi
city-state
oral history
dig
site
theodolite
square
surplus
kiln
ancestor
surveying
grid
trephination
infrared
excavation
scribes
nomads
empires
epic
polytheism
Assyrians
analysis
civilization
genus

Words Within Words

Here is a chalkboard game that can be played over and over again just by changing the initial word. A sample lesson follows, along with directions for making your own word game.

Write the word **archaeology** on the chalkboard or overhead projector for all to see. Direct the students to take out a sheet of scrap paper and a pencil. Tell them to copy the word onto their paper. Explain that all the answers to the clues you are about to give them are all contained in the letters of the word archaeology. Demonstrate this example. First, read aloud this clue: "This is the written record of a ship's progress." Have them guess the answer. Explain that the answer is **log;** the letters l, o, g are contained in the word archaeology.

When everyone is clear about the directions, read the first clue aloud. Have the students raise one hand when they have written an answer on their scrap paper. Choose one student to write his/her response on the chalkboard or overhead projector. Repeat the process for the remaining clues. If the students need help, tell them the number of letters in the answer or supply them with the first letter of the word.

Archaeology Clues and Answers

1. a pain in the stomach (ache)

2. an assigned job (chore)

3. another name for rabbit (hare)

4. an antonym for late (early)

5. folk tales or folk___ (lore)

6. a measure of land (acre)

7. lukewarm (cool)

8. a jealous _____ (rage)

9. a part of a curve (arc)

10. sacred (holy)

11. a plan for the future (goal)

12. another word for genuine (real)

13. to stare intensely (glare)

14. fit for a king; royal (regal)

15. bashful or shy (coy)

16. prayer said before meals (grace)

17. Instead of paying cash some people _____ it. (charge)

18. a shoe with a thick, wooden sole (clog)

19. Ancient humans wrote on this type of tablet. (clay)

20. study of organisms and their relationship to the environment (ecology)

To create your own word game, choose a multi-syllabic word (preferably one that is related to the unit studies). Make a list of all the smaller words you can find within that word. Write clues for the words. As a challenge to students, have them choose a word and write clues; let them present it to the class or a small group.

Reading a Label

Some of our information about ancient humans comes to us through written sources such as cave paintings and clay tablets. Today we are creating written sources for archaeologists of the future. Newspapers, books, magazines, and even food labels will provide the generations to come with information about the way we lived.

Pretend you are an archaeologist of the future and you have found this soup can label. Examine it carefully and then answer the questions that follow.

Nutrition information per serving

Serving size	9.5oz. (269 g)
Servings per container	2
Calories	130
Protein (grams)	4
Carbohydrate (grams)	25
Fat (grams)	2
Sodium	760mg/serving

Percentage of U.S. Recommended Daily Allowances

Protein	6	Riboflavin	15
Vitamin A	150	Niacin	10
Vitamin C	*	Calcium	6
Thiamine	4	Iron	6

*Contains less than 2% of the U.S. RDA of this nutrient.

Ingredients: Chicken stock, potatoes, carrots, celery, water, tomatoes, corn, peas, green beans, potato starch, high fructose corn syrup, yeast extract, salt, dehydrated onions, vegetable oil, disodium inosinate, disodium guanylate, spice extract, dehydrated garlic and chives.

Mama's Home Cooking

Garden Vegetable Soup

Chunks of garden veggies cooked in flavorful broth
Directions: Do not add water.
Stove: Pour soup into saucepan; heat slowly until hot.
Microwave: Pour soup in a microwave-safe bowl. Cover; microwave on high 3.5 minutes.

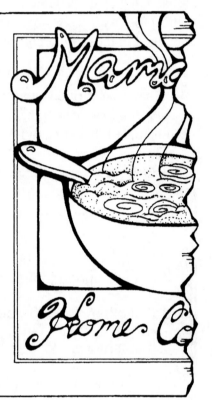

1. How did these people cook their food?

2. Were these people health-conscious?

3. How many servings did this can contain?

4. Which ingredient is less than 2% of the RDA?

5. Are all of the ingredients fresh?

6. Why is disodium inosinate used in this soup?

7. What vitamins does this soup contain?

8. What does dehydrated mean?

9. What are the directions for cooking the soup on the stove?

10. How is the soup cooked in a microwave?

11. What is a microwave?

12. How many calories are in the whole can?

13. How many grams does the whole can weigh?

14. What percentage of Vitamin A does this soup contain?

15. How many grams of sodium are there in the whole can?

16. What fresh vegetables are in this soup?

For Discussion: Do you think the description of soup on the label is misleading or accurate? Based on the list of ingredients what would you name this soup?

     64

What If...

These ten open-ended questions will help students strengthen their critical thinking skills, enhance their research skills, and motivate their creativity. Use the queries for group discussions or writing assignments. A different question can be assigned daily or you may want to supply students with the whole list so they can choose their own topics.

What if...

...you discovered fire while rubbing two dry sticks together. Describe your initial reactions—are you frightened, surprised, excited, etc.? What possible uses would fire have for you and your people?

...an unexpected mudslide buries your house and its contents. Two hundred years later the site is dug up by archaeologists. Tell which artifacts in your house will have survived; explain why. What might have happened to any bodies buried in the mudslide?

...on a trip to Rosetta, Egypt you have found a giant, basalt stone. On it is a message engraved in three different languages—Greek, demotic, and hieroglyphics. Fortunately, you are thoroughly familiar with the Greek language. Explain how you would decode the other two. Which would be easier to decode, the demotic or hieroglyphics?

...you are an African shaman. Describe some charms or amulets used to ward off evil spirits. Tell how you communicate with the spirits. Explain how you use a snake and some bones to foretell the future.

...while on a dig you have just uncovered a small skeleton. What is the age and sex of this skeleton? How can you tell? One member of the dig thinks the skeleton may have suffered from rickets; how can you be sure?

...you and a friend are hiking. You cross a peat bog only to stumble on some bones of a fully preserved mammoth. Also nearby is a large stone knife and a chopper. With these clues in mind, tell what you think might have happened to the mammoth.

...the professor's time machine malfunctioned and a Neanderthal human was brought into this century. What inventions and technologies do you think would impress him/her most? How would you communicate? Do you think he/she would be happy here now?

...you could interview an older person who had lived in your town since he/she was born. What questions would you ask about the changes that have occurred over the years?

...while exploring in your grandparents' attic, you found an old steamer trunk containing tap shoes, a cane, a straw hat, a vest, and an old newspaper clipping. What do you think these artifacts could tell you about their owner?

...you were transported back to the Ice Age. What household items and personal possessions would you miss most? How do you think you would fit in with others your own age?

Squares

A square is the basic unit of measurement used by archaeologists on a dig. Learn more about squares with any of these activities.

Making a Square

Each student will need a sheet of standard-size notebook paper or construction paper and a pair of scissors. (This exercise can be done without scissors, too.)

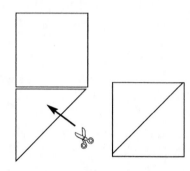

* Fold the paper by placing the short end against the longer side of the paper. (See diagram.)
* With the scissors, cut the rectangular piece from the end of the paper. (If you do not want to use scissors, fold the rectangular piece down and then back up a number of times. Place a ruler along the crease and tear off the piece.)
* Open up the paper to see the square.

Square Numbers

Establish that square numbers are numbers times themselves (e.g., 6x6, 15x15, 7x7). Write the symbol for squared on the board (2). When that symbol is placed above a number, it means that the number should be multiplied by itself.

* Draw an array (an orderly arrangement of numbers in rows or columns) to illustrate a square number. Direct the students to draw a square number of their choice.
* Instruct the students to write the numbers from 1 to 100 on a sheet of paper with 10 numbers across and 10 down. Circle all the square numbers. For a real challenge have them find all the square numbers from 100 to 200 (or more).

Characteristics

Examine some of the unique characteristics of squares. Group the students and direct them to write a list of all the characteristics of a square. Compare lists in the whole class. Establish information such as the following:

* A square is a quadrilateral whose sides are all equal in length.
* The perimeter of a square can be found by multiplying the length of one side by four; the area by multiplying the length of one side times itself.
* All the angles of a square are right angles (90 degrees).
* A square is a rectangle with congruent sides.

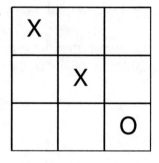

Practical Uses

Discuss some practical applications of squares. Examples include: One carpentry tool is a square; find out how this tool is used. Graph paper is made up of squares; explain why squares are used, not triangles or circles. Square dancing is fun; find out why it is called "square" dancing. Some floor tiles are square; what is the advantage of using this shape? Name some games played on gameboards made up of squares (checkers, chess, tic-tac-toe, etc.).

66

Name_____

Plot the Artifacts

On a mythical dig eight different artifacts were found. You will be able to find the artifacts, too, by plotting their locations on the graph below. After finding a set of directions on the map, circle the point. Then draw a picture of the artifact by the circle. One has already been done for you.

| coins *(W4,S8)* | statue *(N11,E8)* | arrowhead *(S3,E6)* | bones *(N7,W10)* |
| potshards *(E11,N6)* | helmet *(W12,S10)* | mosaic *(N3,W5)* | bolla *(S9,E10)* |

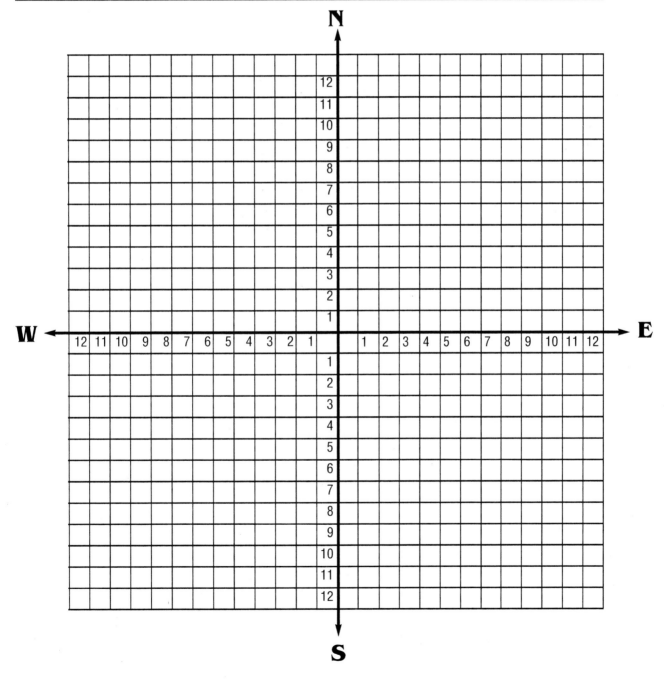

Stratigraphy

Archaeologists begin searching for clues about the past by examining the surface of a site and then proceeding to excavate the land. The site's surface is divided into squares with grids; then, layer by layer, the earth is carefully removed. As objects are found, their exact location is recorded.

The study of these remains in the layers or strata of the earth is called stratigraphy. Geologists read these layers to determine the age of a site and the manner in which stones, bones, and artifacts have been preserved.

Pictured below is a sample cross-section of a site. Label the layers with the following dates: c. 1400 B.C., c. 4000 B.C., and c. 100 B.C. Draw some potshards, coins, and arrowheads in the appropriate layers.

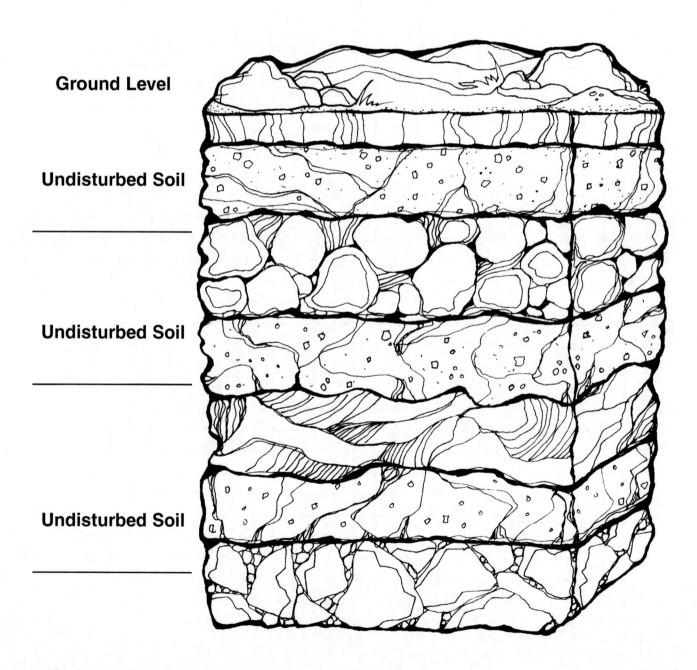

Ground Level

Undisturbed Soil

_____

Undisturbed Soil

_____

Undisturbed Soil

_____

Pioneer Archaeologists

Archaeology was not always the organized, exacting science that it is today. In fact, when earlier ruins were uncovered (such as those at Pompeii) they were only used to unearth statues and other treasures. Over time, the real value of these ancient finds was realized, and archaeology was elevated to a new status.

Many men and women were responsible for bringing archaeology to its current scientific level. Some of them are listed in the box below. Read the descriptions underneath the box and then write the name of the correct archaeologist on the line provided.

> **Thomas Jefferson   John Aubrey   Sir Leonard Woolley   Mary Leakey**
> **Howard Carter   Louis Leakey   Hiram Bingham   Dame Kathleen Kenyon**
> **Augustus Lane-Fox Pitt-Rivers   Sir W.M. Flinders Petrie**

1. _____ A seventeenth-century Englishman, he was an early "field archaeologist" who described the 56 holes surrounding the stone circle at Stonehenge.

2. _____ Because of her excavations in the Laetoli volcanic beds, it was proven that hominids had walked erect over three million years ago.

3. _____ This American archaeologist was born in 1875 and died in 1956. He located the lost city of the Inca—Machu Picchu—in Peru.

4. _____ He was both an archaeologist and an Egyptologist. This Britain also established basic field excavation techniques and invented a sequence dating system.

5. _____ The third president of the U.S.A., he dug up a Native American grave site in Virginia. His work was carried out with precise observation, which was uncommon at the time.

6. _____ One of the greatest cities of ancient Mesopotamia—the Sumerian city of Ur—was unearthed during his excavations in the 1920's.

7. _____ This female British archaeologist excavated Jericho in the Jordan River valley of the Middle East.

8. _____ Both a soldier and an archaeologist, he was one of the first to study stratigraphy. His work was done carefully, and he also drew pictures of everything he unearthed.

9. _____ The Earl of Carnarvon paid for eight years of work to search for the missing tomb of Tutankhamun. Finally, in 1922 it was found by this British archaeologist.

10. _____ A Kenyan archaeologist and anthropologist who, together with his wife, discovered fossils which have been important in learning about the origins of human life.

Archaeological Simulations

To give students a better understanding of life in prehistoric times, provide them with any or all of the following experiences. Activities can be completed on an individual or group basis.

1. **Necklaces.** Cro-Magnon humans made necklaces from shells, fishbones, seeds, and fruit pits. Make your own necklace with a needle and thread and any combination of the materials listed above. Thread the needle, tie a knot in one end of the thread, and push the needle through one item at a time. As an item is added, push it toward the knotted end of the thread. When finished, tie the two ends of the thread together securely and wear the necklace.

2. **Engravings.** Ice Age humans drew paintings on the walls of caves. Create cave paintings with a bar of soap and some simple tools such as a nail file, a paper clip, or a stone. Etch your design into the soap using any of the tools listed. Share your cave painting with your family.

3. **Grain.** Early humans ground grain on a quern or flat stone with a small, round sandstone. Find a large, flat stone and a small round one. Place a handful of grain—wheat, rice, or other grain—on the flat surface. With the small stone, grind the grain against the large stone until the grain is powdery.

4. **Seals.** The Sumerians designed delicately carved stone seals which were pressed into wet clay. This resulted in raised pictures which designated ownership. To make your own raised pictures, roll out prepared sugar cookie dough or clay or homemade clay*. Press cookie cutters with raised designs into the dough or clay. Bake the cookies or allow the dough to dry.

5. **Pictographs.** One of the greatest contributions of the Sumerians was the invention of a system of writing called pictographs. These pictures stood for words or ideas and were drawn on moist clay with a stylus. Roll a rectangular piece of clay to at least one-fourth inch (.6 cm) thick. On the clay, use a wood cuticle stick (or other tool) to draw pictographs of some words you encounter every day (school, books, food, etc.).

6. **Food.** Prehistoric humans enjoyed a varied diet. Some of their foods even included plants that are now considered weeds by most people. Try some of the foods from the list that follows: dandelion leaves, juniper berries, sunflower seeds, almonds, hazelnuts, mint, sage, peppercorns, salmon, dates, figs, and basil. Be adventurous and try a food that you have never eaten before.

7. **Jewelry.** Simple bent-metal links were connected to form necklaces in the Bronze Age. Make your own linked necklace or bracelet with metal pop can tabs or the plastic squares that are used to seal loaves of bread or plastic bags.

*For an easy-to-make clay recipe see page 21.

Research Topics

Listed on this page are a number of topics that students can choose from for further study. You may assign oral or written reports based on these subjects or any others that you may want to add to the list.

* Numismatics (the study of coins, particularly those from ancient times)

* Daily life in Cro-Magnon or Neanderthal times

* Hammurabi's Code and its impact on today's laws

* Early Tools—how they were constructed, how they were used

* Ancient monuments such as Stonehenge, the pyramids of Egypt or Mexico and Central America

* Mt. Vesuvius and the destruction of Pompeii

* Time line of important events in the Ice Age

* The work of Louis and Mary Leakey

* A pictorial of clothing through the ages

* Prehistoric food—a typical diet

* A comparison of the Homo habilis and Homo erectus

* The importance of the discovery of fire

* Art work in the Ice Age, particularly Lascaux, France or Altamira, Spain

* Exploration of burial methods through the ages

* Cuneiforms, hieroglyphs, and other forms of ancient writing

* Currency and other forms of money

* A chart of some methods of weights and measurements

* List and description of tools used by archaeologists

* Life in Ur or Catal Huyuk or other early civilization

* A comparison of radiocarbon dating versus potassium-argon dating

* Diagram of a prehistoric village

* A discussion of the evidences of trade among early cities

* Early farming and the rise of cities

* Early methods of food storage

Terms to Know

This list may be used as a beginning study guide for students. Add to it throughout the archaeology unit.

Archaeologist: A scientist who studies how people lived hundreds and thousands of year ago.

Artifacts: Objects made by humans, e.g., coins, clothing, tools.

Archaeological Site: A place where ancient people lived, worked, or left things they made—e.g., the pyramids of Egypt.

Culture: The total way of life of a particular group including its art, literature, religion, philosophy, sports, clothing, politics, and customs.

Cultural Dating: The process used by archaeologists when they compare objects they find with information they already have.

Cultural Diffusion: The process in which different cultures come in contact with one another and exchange goods and ideas.

Dendrochronology: The oldest form of scientific dating; tree-ring counting.

Digs: Places where archaeologists dig to search for ancient artifacts, buildings, and cities.

Excavation: The process of digging up the remains of the past.

Fossils: The remains or imprints of once-living plants and animals.

Midden: Ancient people's rubbish.

Oral Tradition: Legends, myths, and beliefs passed on by word of mouth from generation to generation.

Potassium-Argon Dating: The technique used to determine the age of inorganic material, usually volcanic rocks.

Prehistory: History before the development of writing.

Primary Sources: Sources produced during the same time period as the events they describe.

Radiocarbon Dating: The technique in which the radioactive carbon content of an archaeological discovery is measured to determine the object's age.

Secondary Sources: Materials created at a later time by people who studied original sources.

Stratigraphy: The study of the remains that are found in various layers of soil and rock.

Making Mosaics

Let students choose which of the following mosaics they would like to create. If you can, prepare a sample of each project on this page. Copy the directions below and cut apart; laminate for more durability. Place the corresponding directions with the proper art project at an art center or other area set aside for making art works. Students can read the directions and complete their own designs.

Tissue Paper Mosaics

Materials: white glue thinned with water; paintbrushes; art tissue paper cut or torn into tiny square pieces; white construction paper; pencils.

Directions:

* With the pencil, lightly draw an outline of a design onto the construction paper background.

* Dip the paintbrush into the glue, and, with the wet tip pick up a piece of art tissue.

* Place the tissue on the design. Brush the tissue piece with glue.

* Continue in the same manner until the entire design has been covered with tissue paper squares.

Clay Mosaics

Materials: clay or homemade clay (For recipe, see page 21.); broken pieces of colored glass or plastic, marbles, etc.; toothpick; string.

Directions:

* Flatten the clay or dough to the desired size and shape. (For best results, the clay should be about one-half inch/1.3 cm thick).

* Press pieces of the glass, plastic, and the marbles into the surface of the clay.

* With the toothpick prepare a hole through the top of the clay.

* When the clay mosaic is dry, thread string through the hole. Hang and display.

Edible Mosaics

Materials: miniature gumdrops; scissors; prepared frosting; graham crackers; plastic knives.

Directions:

* With the scissors, cut the gumdrops in halves, fourths, or various shapes.

* Use the knife to spread the frosting onto the graham crackers.

* Arrange the pieces of gumdrops onto the crackers in a mosaic design.

* After judging for most intricate design or other category, eat the art.

One Square at a Time

Drawing is easy if you do it one square at a time. Look at the picture in the left graph below. Choose one square and notice the drawn outline in that square. Use coordinates, such as, b,2 etc., to help you find that same square in the blank graph on the right. Once you have located the correct square on the blank graph, copy that portion of the drawing onto the space. Continue in the same manner until the picture is completed. Add a scene or figures to your urn.

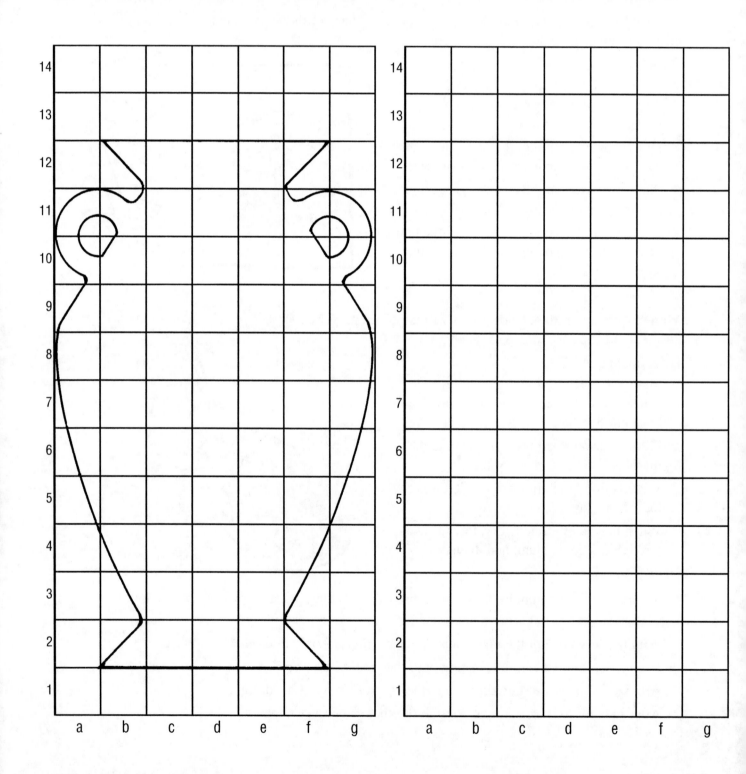

Bulletin Board Ideas

Presented on this page are a number of ideas to help you get started in creating your own bulletin board for an archaeology unit. Adapt these suggestions to conform to your own classroom needs.

Currently in Archaeology

Line a bulletin board background with colored butcher paper. Make a simple border out of newspaper strips. (See diagram.) Write an appropriate title directly onto the butcher paper background or on a strip of construction paper which is then attached to the bulletin board. Suggested titles include: Currently in Archaeology; Archaeology Today; Digging for News in Archaeology; Old but New, etc. Tell students to bring in newspaper articles, magazine stories, etc. about archaeological topics. Share them with the class before attaching them to the bulletin board. Continue to add to the display throughout the unit.

Classroom Door

Don't overlook the classroom door as a possible bulletin board. Tape colored butcher paper to the inside of the door for a background. (Items can also be taped directly to the door if their removal will not destroy the paint.) Print a block letter title onto the paper background and draw dots on the ends of each letter. (See the diagram.) If working directly onto the door, attach cut-out letters vertically as shown. Use to display a group project, outstanding work, special projects, creative writing, etc.

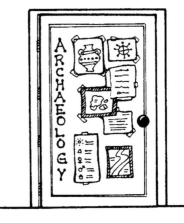

Recyclable Bulletin Board

For this display surface, you will need a large sheet of colored posterboard (available at art supply stores). With a wide marking pen write a title directly onto the board. Laminate for more durability. (If your school laminator cannot accommodate a sheet of posterboard that size, check with a local teacher book and supply store.) Write on the laminated surface with water-based, wipe-off markers. Use this bulletin board to list weekly spelling or vocabulary words, to post a math problem of the day, or to record the results of a brainstorming session. For easy viewing, stand up the bulletin board on the chalkboard tray; or, before laminating punch two holes on either side at the top of the posterboard. Attach clear hole reinforcers on both sides of the holes. Laminate and run a length of string or yarn through the holes so that the bulletin board can be hung from the classroom ceiling. (See diagram at left.)

Awards

Let it be known that

_____

(student's name)

is hereby cited for satisfactory completion of
archaeological studies.

_____   _____
Date   **Teacher's Signature**

Congratulations

to

_____

(student's name)

on a successful dig into the study of ARCHAEOLOGY.

_____   _____
Date   **Teacher's Signature**

Etc.

Included on this page are a number of mixed-media resources that you might want to explore and employ throughout the archaeology unit. Check your school and public libraries for availability of some of these items. Others may be found at video stores.

Calliope: World History for Young People

Cobblestone Publishing, Inc.

7 School Street

Petersborough, NH 03458

This magazine focuses on a different theme each issue. It is published five times during the school year.

(*Cobblestone* and *Faces* are two more magazines printed by the same publishers above; both of these magazines are appropriate for grades 4 - 9.)

National Geographic World

P.O. Box 2174

Washington, D.C. 20013

This is the junior version of *National Geographic Magazine*, but it is every bit as informative.

Archaeology

Archaeological Institute of America

15 Park Row

New York, NY 10038

Although this magazine is geared for adult readers, students may find this official publication of the American Institute of Archaeology to be a good resource.

The Pyramid Explorer's Kit

Running Press, 1991

125 South 22nd Street

Philadelphia, PA 19103

1-800-345-5359

The emphasis in this hands-on learning kit is to assemble a replica of the Great Pyramid at Giza. First, however, pyramid blocks buried in the clay provided must be "excavated."

Everything We Know About Archaeology for You to Use in Your Classroom

National Park Service

800 North Capitol Street N.W.

Suite 210

Washington, D.C. 20002

Archaeological Assistance Division

P.O. Box 37127

Washington, D.C. 20013

This resource guide is available for teachers by writing to the address listed above.

Ancient Empires

The Learning Company

Call 1-800-852-2255 for more information.

Children ages ten and up will enjoy this action adventure computer game which emphasizes decision-making and strategic thinking skills.

Interact

by Jerry Lipetzky

Interact

P.O. Box 997-S2-91

Lakeside, CA 92040

Sixth to ninth grade students will enjoy the dig simulation activities provided in this guide.

Answer Key *(cont.)*

page 19
1. Choose the site...
2. Examine the site...
3. Determine the number...
4. Look for pottery...
5. Survey and draw up...
6. Place each find...
7. At day's end,...
8. Wash and dry the...
9. Mark each piece...
10. Use all the artifacts....

page 20
1. lute, lyre
2. strata, silt
3. aqueduct, ziggurat
4. cuneiform, heiroglyphs, pictograph
5. mosaic, sherds, urns
6. bacteria, fungi, chemicals, pollution
7. trowel, theodolite, sieve
8. mummification, peat bogs, volcanoes
9. dendrochronology, carbon-14, thermoluminescence, potassium-argon
10. sonic helmet, aqualung

page 23
1. 25 sq. m
2. 108 cu. ft.
3. 144 in; 12 ft.
4. 600
5. 24 cu. ft.
6. 11 m
7. 9 in.
8. 8 m

page 25
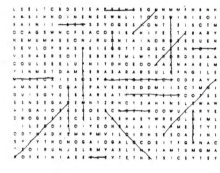

page 26
1. Neanderthal
2. Homo habilis
3. Cro-Magnon
4. Neanderthal
5. Cro-Magnon
6. Homo erectus
7. Homo habilis, Homo erectus, Neanderthal
8. Cro-Magnon
9. Homo erectus
10. Homo habilis, Homo erectus

page 27

page 28
1. epigrapher
2. botanist
3. artist
4. geologists
5. paleontologists
6. ceramist
7. photographer
8. zoologist
9. registrar
10. anthropologist

page 32
Egypt, Red Sea, Mesopotamia, Indian Ocean, Indus, China, 1. Atlantic Ocean, 2. Gulf of Mexico 3. Mesoamerica, 4. Pacific Ocean, 5. South America, 6. Roman Republic, 7 Mycenae, 8. Mediterranean Sea, 9. Egypt, 10. Africa, 11. China, 12. Indus, 13. Arabian Sea, 14. Indian Ocean

page 37
dark rings, ring patterns, counting rings Carbon Dating: carbon 14, living organisms, half-life, date up to 50,000 years
Obsidian Hydration: natural glass, absorbs water, rapidly cooling lava, hydration or thickness
Thermo-luminescence: clay, stores energy, reheat excavated potsherds, measures amount of light

page 38
Check for appropriate responses.

page 39
Minoans: settled on Crete, flourished between 2000 B.C. and 1400 B.C., earliest civilization of Europe, produced wine and olive oil, richly painted and decorated houses, kept a sizable navy, not fortified against attack
Both: sailed the Mediterranean, Greek in origin, traded goods with other settlements

Mycenaeans: developed near Athens; warriors; flourished between 1600 B.C. to 1400 B.C.; decorated pottery with weapons; Iliad and Odyssey set in this period; buried their dead with daggers, swords, and shields; dead were placed in huge domed tombs

page 42
1. Napoleon Bonaparte
2. Heinrich Schliemann
3. Flinders Petrie
4. Charles Darwin
5. Johann Winckelmann
6. Georg Grotefund
7. Howard Carter
8. Arthur Evans
9. Jean-Francois Champollion
10. Augustus Pitt-Rivers
11. Giuseppe Fiorelli
12. Otto I

Answer Key *(cont.)*

page 43

1. 4000 - 2300 = 1700 yrs.
2. 237 x 110 = 26,070 sq. ft.
3. 20,000 divided by 5 = 4000 people/sq. mi.
4. 1906 + 35 = 1941
5. 237 x 110 x 60 = 1,564,200 cu.ft.
6. 2144 - 2124 = 20 yrs.
7. 1728 - 79 = 1,649 years
8. square root of 9 mi. = 3 mi.
9. 200 - 60 = 140 ft.
10. 2 x 110 + 2 x 237 = 220 + 474 = 694 ft.

page 46

1. Turkey
2. plateau
3. plain
4. Sumer
5. city-state
6. artisan
7. epic
8. nomads
9. polytheism
10. alphabet
11. empire
12. code
13. ziggurat
14. wheel
15. bulla

page 47

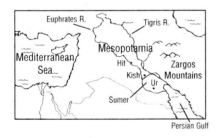

page 48

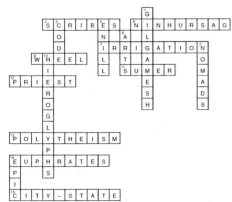

page 49

1. stable food supply
2. specialization of labor
3. system of government
4. social levels
5. highly developed culture that includes art, religion, music, & law

page 51

The ancient Sumerians and Mesopotamians used clay tablets to record all kinds of information on every topic imaginable.

page 52

1. cause: irrigation allowed farmers...
   effect: Sumer gave rise...
2. cause: there was a surplus of food
   effect: Some people were able...
3. cause: they needed to transport goods..
   effect: The Sumerians invented...
4. cause: The Sumerians felt helpless...
   effect: they tried their best to...
5. cause: Because of very little rain...
   effect: the Sumerians created an...
6. cause: they needed an accurate method..
   effect: Writing was invented...

page 64

1. on the stove; in the microwave
2. yes—nutrition information is printed on the label
3. two
4. Vitamin C
5. no, some are dried
6. as a preservative or flavor-enhancer
7. Vitamins A and C
8. the water has been removed
9. Pour soup into saucepan; heat slowly until hot.
10. Pour soup in a microwave-safe bowl. Cover; microwave on high 3.5 minutes.
11. a type of oven
12. 260
13. 538 gm
14. 150
15. 1520
16. potatoes, carrots, celery, tomatoes, corn, peas, green beans

page 68

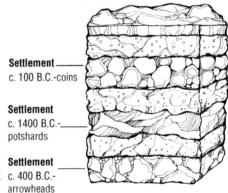

page 69

1. John Aubrey
2. Mary Leakey
3. Hiram Bingham
4. Sir W.M. Flinders Petrie
5. Thomas Jefferson
6. Sir Leonard Woolley
7. Dame Kathleen Kenyon
8. August Lane-Fox Pitt-Rivers
9. Howard Carter
10. Louis Leakey

Bibliography

Fiction

Alexander, Lloyd. *The Illyrian Adventure*. Dutton, 1986.

Baumann, Hans. *In the Land of Ur.* Pantheon Books, 1969.

Behn, Harry. *The Faraway Lurs.* Gregg Press, 1981.

Feagles, Anita. *He Who Saw Everything.* (The Epic of Gilgamesh.) Young Scott Books, 1966.

James, Carollyn. *Digging Up the Past: The Story of an Archaeological Adventure.* Franklin Watts, 1990.

Kittleman, Laurence. *Canyons Beyond the Sky.* Atheneum, 1985.

McHargue, Georges. *The Turquoise Toad Mystery.* Delacorte, 1982.

Peretti, Frank E. *The Door in the Dragon's Throat.* Good News, 1985.

Van Loon, Hendrick Willem. *The Story of Mankind.* Liveright, 1985.

Wells, Rosemary. *Through the Hidden Door.* Dial, 1987.

Nonfiction

Anderson, Joan. *From Map to Museum: Uncovering Mysteries of the Past.* Morrow, 1988.

Barry, Iris. *Discovering Archaeology.* Stonehenge Press Inc., 1981 (printed in the U.S.A. by Rand McNally & Co.).

Branigan, Keith. *Prehistory.* Franklin Watts, 1986.

Cooke, Jean, et al. *Archaeology.* Bookwright Press, 1987.

Cork, Barbara and Struan Reid. *The Usborne Young Scientist: Archaeology.* Usborne Publishing, 1984.

Dunrea, Olivier. *Skara Brae: The Story of a Prehistoric Village.* Holiday House, 1986.

Fortiner, Virginia J. *The Science-Hobby Book of Archaeology.* Lerner Publications, 1974.

Fradin, Dennis B. *Archaeology.* Childrens, 1983.

Glubok, Shirley. *Art and Archaeology.* Harper, 1986.

Hackwell, W. John. *Digging to the Past: Excavations in Ancient Lands.* Macmillan, 1986.

  Diving to the Past. Charles Scribner's Sons, 1988.

  Signs, Letters, Words: Archaeology Discovers Writing. Macmillan,1987.

Lampton, Christopher. *Undersea Archaeology.* Franklin Watts, 1988.

Lasky, Kathryn. *Traces of Life.* Morrow Junior Books, 1989.

Leroi-Gourhan, Andre. *The Hunters of Prehistory*. Atheneum, 1989.

Marston, Elsa. *Mysteries in American Archaeology.* Walker, 1986.

Merriman, Nick. *Eyewitness Books: Early Humans.* Dorling Kindersley, 1989.

Millon, Bill. *Archaeology Handbook: A Field Manual and Resource Guide.* John Wiley and Sons, 1991.

Morrison, Velma Ford. *Going on a Dig.* Dodd, Mead & Company, 1981.

Moss, Carol. *Science in Ancient Mesopotamia.* Franklin Watts, 1988.

Pickering, Robert B. *I Can Be an Archaeologist.* Childrens Press, 1987.

Porell, Bruce. *Digging the Past: Archaeology in Your Own Backyard.* Harper, 1979.

Rollin, Sue. *The Illustrated Atlas of Archaeology.* Warwick Press, 1982.

Steele, William O. *Talking Bones: Secrets of Indian Mound Builders.* Harper, 1978 .

Stein, Sara. *The Evolution Book.* Workman, 1986.

Williams, Barbara. *Breakthrough: Women in Archaeology.* Walker, 1991.